Fodor's

HOW TO PACK

Experts Share

Their SECRETS

BY LAUREL CARDONE

Fodor's Travel Publications, Inc.
New York • Toronto • London • Sydney • Auckland
www.fodors.com/

Fodor's HOW TO PACK

Editors: Holly Hughes, Karen Cure
Editorial Contributors: Audra Epstein, Allison Hartmann
Production Editorial: Linda K. Schmidt
Production/Manufacturing: Robert B. Shields
Creative Director: Fabrizio La Rocca
Text and Cover Design: Guido Caroti
Illustrations: Alida Beck

COPYRIGHT

SPECIAL SALES

Fodor's Travel Publications are available at special discounts for bulk purchases for sales promotions or premiums. Special editions, including personalized covers, excerpts of existing guides, and corporate imprints, can be created in large quantities for special needs. For more information, contact your local bookseller or write to Special Markets, Fodor's Travel Publications, 201 East 50th Street, New York, NY 10022. Inquiries from Canada should be directed to your local Canadian bookseller or sent to Random House of Canada, Ltd., Marketing Department, 1265 Aerowood Drive, Mississauga, Ontario L4W 1B9. Inquiries from the United Kingdom should be sent to Fodor's Travel Publications, 20 Vauxhall Bridge Road, London, England SW1V 2SA.

PRINTED IN THE UNITED STATES OF AMERICA

ACKNOWLEDGMENTS

Many thanks to travel pros Steve Margolies and Pete Weis, and to the Luggage and Leather Goods Manufacturers of America.

Thanks also to my wonderful family and friends for their support, encouragement—and packing stories!

Contents

	INTRODUCTION	vi
1	HOW TO BUY LUGGAGE	1

Look at Your Needs 3
Suitcases for All Travel Styles 5
Pullmans 5
Duffels 9
Garment Bags 12
Travel Packs 14
Laptop Luggage 17
To Wheel or Not to Wheel? 19
Are You a Carry-On Traveler? 21
How to Judge Quality 28

2	PRIME PACKING PRINCIPLES	35

The Advance Planning 37
Lay the Groundwork 37
Get Busy and Get It Done 42
Make a Travel Kit 45
A Toiletries Kit 45
The Sewing Kit 52
The First-Aid Kit 54
The Personal Documents Kit 55
The Portable Office 56
For Passionate Shoppers 57
The Toy Tote 58
Countdown to Packing 61
The Night Before 64
Get Packing! 66
How to Fill Almost Any Suitcase 66
For Duffels and Travel Packs 73
Know-How for Garment Baggers 74
Practically Crease-Free Folding 79
Packing Carry-Ons 83

3   THE PACKING LIST   88

Your Wardrobe **89**
Packing Pointers **94**
Active Trips and Adventures *94*
Business Trips and Seminars *102*
Casual Vacations *104*
City Vacations *106*
Cruises *108*
For Families *109*
Resort Vacations *112*

4   HOW TO PACK FOR THE WAY BACK   114

Use Your Packing List *115*
Dirty Laundry *116*
The Paper Chase *117*
Souvenir Savvy *118*
At Customs *121*

APPENDIX:
LUGGAGE & PACKING RESOURCES   122

WHAT MAKES A PACKING PRO?

"A journey of a thousand miles must begin with a single step," said Lao-tzu, the 6th-century BC philosopher. It's a lovely sentiment. But for most travelers, the first step is packing. And packing is more like a giant leap across a yawning chasm. An hour before leaving for the airport, they pull out a suitcase bought 10 years ago, blow into it, turn it over, shake it, and pronounce it garment ready. Then they pull out a bureau drawer and upend the contents into the suitcase. On top goes an iron, to eliminate wrinkles upon arrival.

Sitting on the suitcase to force it shut, wrestling with the fasteners, many of these same people swear there's got to be a better way. And there is.

You go to your closet and choose, from an extensive luggage collection, a bag that's just the right size for the trip, one that's loaded with nifty compartments that will keep clothing organized on the road. You line it with crisp, clean tissue paper and fill it strategically—guided by a carefully edited packing list prepared during the preceding two or three weeks—with freshly washed and ironed or dry-cleaned garments, each one carefully encased in plastic, shoes bagged and tidily filled with rolled undergarments and incidentals, and a toiletry kit that contains everything you need. The suitcase closes easily; nothing is left behind; and everything arrives as bandbox fresh as it was in your closet.

If you aspire to this vision, this book is for you.

This book will help you start a luggage wardrobe if you haven't already. It will help you expand your luggage wardrobe if you need to.

It will also help you with the critical planning that makes packing a breeze.

My advice takes into account the practical realities of travel and of human nature. While some pretrip packing strategies can be downright compulsive, I'm here to tell you about a few that can be real lifesavers, even for the shortest, most last-minute journey. Frequent travelers (and there are more and more of us these days) have plenty of tried-and-true tricks that pay off every time you travel. Some of these techniques save time, others save money, and still others save suitcase space and weight. (It's a wonderful feeling, being able to stroll right off the plane with an ultra-light carry-on and go straight to the taxi stand, miles ahead of your fellow passengers.) Other tips pay off at your destination, when you find that you've got everything you need (and nothing more)—your clothes look great, everything matches, and your shoes don't hurt.

And here's the beautiful part: You can start getting ready now, even if you have no specific trip in the offing.

Different trips require different strategies, of course. The length of your journey, the season you're traveling in, the itinerary, the purpose of your trip, your mode of travel, whom you're traveling with—all must be factored in. I'll show you how to analyze your needs beforehand, so that you'll have the right suitcase and the right packing list every time. After all, you don't need the same clothes for a week's hike in the Rockies that you do for a long weekend at a resort in Bermuda or a fortnight's theater-going in London.

As a travel journalist who's often on the road, I've honed my methods gradually. I've learned a lot from fellow travelers, whose pearls of wisdom I'll pass on to you. I've also learned a lot, I have to admit, from my own mistakes—as you'll see in the chapters that follow. Reading this book should spare you similar blunders.

One goal is uppermost: to make your packing a simpler first step. So that, bags packed, you can move on to the fun part. Here's to a lifetime of rewarding journeys!

Laurel Cardone
New York, New York

1

HOW TO BUY LUGGAGE

Perhaps you have been staving off the inevitable, borrowing luggage as often as you can, or using those inadequate, dilapidated bags just one more time while vowing you'll replace them before your next trip. Never fear: Somewhere out there is the perfect bag with your name on it.

Dozens of manufacturers produce, each, dozens of styles. And each style comes in several different sizes, often in at least two different fabrics. Flight attendants' rolling carry-ons, which debuted in 1988, spawned a suitcase revolution that can be felt in every corner of the luggage department. The pullman, the rectangular container that has long been synonymous with the word "suitcase," has gone vertical and sprouted wheels and a handle. So have duffels and backpacks—now known as "travel packs." Today's luggage store presents a far different scene from the one you would have encountered 10 years ago, or even 5.

FOUR STEPS TO THE PERFECT SUITCASE

❑ Assess your needs.

❑ Look at other people's luggage.

❑ Shop around—develop a short list.

❑ Compare quality and price.

Look at Your Needs

Recently some friends and I discussed the idea that everyone, consciously or not, has a wish list of qualities for the perfect mate. Consider how much time you spend with your luggage and how intimately you come to know it. Is your choice of suitcase less important than choosing a mate? Do you want your luggage to look attractive, suit your budget, or be ultradurable, light, and portable? After you've decided what's essential, remember that in luggage, as in love, perfection is an illusion—a bag that has most of the qualities that matter to you is probably as close as you'll come. Choosing the right luggage is really just an extension of Philosophy 101: Know thyself, and thou shalt surely know thy luggage.

WHAT TO THINK ABOUT Before you begin to zero in on particular brands and styles, take the time to consider how you like to travel. (And remember to revisit your assessment every few years—career moves, growing families, and changes in income can totally transform your travel habits.)

Consider when, how, and how often you will use the luggage. Do you plan to travel by air? by car? on a train or bus? How frequently do you expect to be taking trips? Do you usually travel alone, with a friend or partner, or with a family?

How frequently and how far will you need to transport your bag? Will you be checking it or lugging it through an airport to the gate as a carry-on piece? Do you think you may carry this suitcase yourself, or are you a person who hails porters whenever possible? Do you usually have a car waiting for you, or are you the sort that prefers public transportation?

What is the nature of your trip? Do you expect to be traveling through several European countries by train, for which mobility will be crucial? Is there a cruise in your future? (You'll unpack the first evening, then kiss your bags goodbye for the duration of the voyage.) Do you take standard hotel trips, where bellhops are always on hand? Do you plan to hike and climb mountains with your luggage? Or will you be on the smooth streets of a big city?

How do you like to carry your luggage? Do you roll it, sling it over your shoulder, or strap it onto your back?

How do you pack? Do you prefer to hang your garments, roll them, or fold them? Do you always take more gear than you need, or do you rigorously prune down your packing list to a few essentials?

A LUGGAGE WARDROBE Think in terms of building a luggage wardrobe. Keep in mind the color, style, and function of the piece or pieces you own already, and make sure new items coordinate and serve a specific purpose. Buy pieces from different manufacturers, or stay with one line you like. While some folks like to buy a whole set of luggage at once, others prefer to purchase an essential piece or two, and then add a new item annually or as needed. The advantage of waiting is that you have an introduction to a line of luggage through your initial purchase; if you aren't pleased with its standards of construction or durability, you won't be stuck fretting over having invested in three other bags from the same manufacturer.

OTHER PEOPLE'S LUGGAGE

Whenever you're traveling, inspect fellow passengers' luggage to see what works. Don't be afraid to ask questions—people actually seem to *like* sharing luggage stories. Is that petite retiree easily trundling along with a massive suitcase on wheels? If so, the wheels and frame must be well designed. Is that stylish duffel on the hotel's luggage cart splitting open at the seams? Depend on it that the stitching and/or fabric just can't hold up under serious traveling.

Suitcases for All Travel Styles

My first piece of luggage must have been the flowered cotton overnight bag that I brought to my cousin Jennifer's sleep-over birthday party. Although the party was only across the street, I was going away for a whole night—who knew what I might need? The bag was perfect for me because, even packed to bursting, it was still small enough for me to shoulder by myself. (My dad carried my sleeping bag and pillow—who says chivalry is dead?) As I grew older, I borrowed my parents' suitcases for trips to upstate New York, Rhode Island, Bermuda...Eventually, I borrowed my brother's big red backpack for a spring trip to Europe. I say "big" because that's what it was—from the top of its shiny exterior aluminum frame to the bottom loops for crampons I would never use, the thing must have stood a good 3½ feet tall, and probably would have seen me through a journey to Nepal. In fact, if I hadn't been so lucky with youth hostels that spring, I probably could've slept inside it. It was so big that when my traveling companions saw it circling anonymously around the baggage carousel, I heard one of them exclaim, "Imagine the poor slob who's got to carry that thing around!"

We live and learn.

When I became a travel writer, I decided it was time for luggage of my own. But which type to buy? I was almost overwhelmed by the choices. I purchased a serious garment bag and a matching cabin bag, both in black nylon with grooved rubber patches, and was instantly transformed. I felt cool. I felt like an adult. I had luggage—there was no place I couldn't go. Thinking about your options in advance will make it a lot easier for you to get there, too.

▶ Pullmans

Long ago, wealthy travelers transported their belongings in hard-sided steamer trunks and hat boxes. But something happened on the way to the 21st century. These

trunks didn't fit into the compact sleeping cars of America's trains, and a new suitcase style was born. A rectangular box with a hinged lid and a handle centered on the long open side, it was known as the pullman, named after the premier manufacturer of sleeping cars. Soon it became the suitcase of choice, and it still is for many travelers. But in almost every airport today, you'll find armies of travelers wheeling so-called vertical pullmans, which open just like the standard pullman but have wheels on one short side, and, on the other, a telescoping handle and a second carrying handle.

Inside most pullmans, depending on the specific model, you'll find features that will help keep your clothing organized. Perfect for business travelers, "suiters" have a special compartment that opens to reveal a hanger bar for a suit or other dress clothes. Depending upon the dimensions of the case, it can accommodate two or three suits or several dresses and jackets. The garments are held in place by either a fabric strap or a padded bar, and the **extra** panel folds over in half or in thirds—which means that your clothing is folded only once or twice, and each fold is padded to prevent creases. On the opposite side, the suitcase opens up to reveal a compartment in which to store shirts, underwear, accessories, and toiletries. A quick change in your hotel room on arrival and you look pressed, polished, and professional.

Other pullmans have simply one large, unstructured space inside, and, as a result, they can accommodate themselves to many packing styles. They work just as well for rolled-up dungarees and T-shirts as for jackets, trousers, blouses, and other easily wrinkled items that are best laid flat. And these pullmans come with wheels and without, and in sizes ranging from humongous to small enough to fit under an airplane seat.

HARD OR SOFT? For years, travelers have debated the comparative virtues of soft- and hard-sided pullmans. Suitcases made of shiny aluminum and of molded materials like polypropylene and ABS plastic have edged out earlier hard-siders, which were traditionally made of cardboard or plywood covered with fabric, leather, or vinyl and bound with leather or vinyl at the seams.

MISSION IMPOSSIBLE

For years, photographers have been packing their expensive camera gear in stylish aluminum boxes. Now manufacturers have added wheels. These modern hard-siders are truly eye-catching; they generally have a silver or gold finish and are both waterproof and fireproof—just the thing for important documents. Aluminum suitcases are sturdy, cannot be slashed open like some fabric bags, and last virtually forever. On the down side, the metal can be scratched and dented, and it makes for a case that is a bit hefty even when empty.

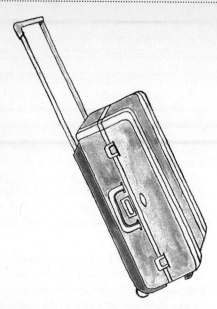

Today's soft-sided versions are made of fabrics ranging from Cordura and other durable synthetics to leather, vinyl made to look like leather, elaborate tapestry nylons, and nylon tweeds; these are usually stretched over a full or partial frame. Which you prefer is entirely a matter of personal preference.

Innovative designs as well as strong, lightweight fabrics have made soft-sided bags as durable as their hard-sided cousins, and they weigh less. Soft-sided luggage tends to be flexible enough to allow you to squeeze in that last precious souvenir; once hard-sided luggage is packed, it's packed. And although soft-sided pieces may appear to be flimsier than hard-sided ones, if they're thrown around (and they will be) they actually absorb shocks better than hard-sided bags. Soft-sided luggage made of good-quality ballistic nylon—this is similar to the stuff used in bulletproof vests—is virtually impossible to puncture or slash (see How to Judge Quality, below). On the other hand, hard-sided pieces offer better protection when crushed or sat upon; if you plan to carry around bisque figurines or other breakables, it's the best choice.

THE ULTIMATE SUITCASE One well-known manufacturer of adventure luggage offers its own, rather nifty convertible version of the standard 22-inch suitcase with wheels: A zip-out panel folds down to cover the wheels, revealing back straps that convert the bag into a travel pack. After all, wheels won't do you much good on a wilderness trail, and what you can't pull you might as well carry on your back.

▶ Duffels

Santa Claus uses a duffel. So do postal workers. So did all those young men in uniform you see in scenes from classic movies; as they share a farewell embrace with loved ones, a heavy canvas bag, stuffed to bursting, stands waiting on the porch.

Duffels have terrific portability. Soft-sided and frameless, they're just right when you're packing casual clothing. They're lighter and cost less than most traditional suitcases. They're easy to carry by hand or over the shoulder. And they're endlessly forgiving when you have a bit too much to pack. As a result, they make excellent vacation bags—many people feel they can pack for a two-week trip in a duffel that slips under an airplane seat. Duffels are especially good when you're traveling with children—their things generally don't need as much protection as adult clothes.

Some duffels also come with wheels, functioning in much the same way as pullmans with wheels. While less expensive models must be dragged by the opposite corner, pricier ones have a telescoping handle. This type of bag still looks sporty, but has a slightly more professional air than a typical duffel.

THE BAG THAT CAN GROW Duffels are sized by cubic inches of space: A typical carry-on model has a capacity of about 2,500 cubic inches, a full-size one of be-

tween 3,500 and 4,500 cubic inches (larger ones are available). But some duffels also have an expansion segment—an extra 5 or 6 inches of space at the end or bottom of the bag that can be freed by zipper so that the bag can "grow" when needed. This is especially handy when you're returning home with more than you originally packed. It also makes for a more flexible piece of luggage; since you can choose which size to use, you don't need two separate bags.

WHAT'S INSIDE Bare-bones duffels generally have a single compartment and no outside pockets. Upscale versions, made of more substantial fabric—ballistic nylon, Cordura, or Cordura Plus—generally have separate compartments at either end for shoes and accessories, and perhaps an outside pocket or two.

Some duffels are equipped with hidden back and waist straps that convert them into travel packs. Easy to carry as a duffel may be when you're walking down the street, it's great to have the option of backpacking when the terrain gets rougher or when you need your hands free (to hold your child's hand, perhaps). Because they don't have frames, these won't be as comfortable as a full-scale travel pack when you're carrying heavy loads, but they can be marvelous in a pinch.

OVER THE RAINBOW In terms of color, duffels have certainly come out of the closet in recent years, even more so than other types of luggage. On a recent trip to a luggage store, I was nearly blinded when I turned from the time-tested neutrals of the other types of bags to the Day-Glo rainbow of duffels. (Conservative travelers take heart—duffels still come in basic black, brown, navy, and green.) Be adventurous, while remembering the colors of your other luggage: A bright-red, safety-orange, or lemon-yellow duffel might look smashing against your black or navy-blue pullman.

LL BEAN'S TIPS ON WHERE TO BUY LUGGAGE

Shopping for quality luggage is more convenient than ever at L.L. Bean. Since 1929, when "L.L." and his son designed the first L.L. Bean luggage collection, we've been building dependable, practical luggage for almost every journey imaginable.

In our stores, and online, you'll find a full selection of duffles, rolling pullmans, shoulder and garment bags, travel packs and briefcases, plus a wide assortment of accessories. All constructed of time-tested fabrics, including long-lasting packcloth, lightweight Micro-fiber™, rugged nylon and oiled Outback leather. At L.L.Bean, we have the right luggage to meet all your travel needs. And, like all our products, our luggage is backed by our 100% guarantee of satisfaction.

ORDER TRAVEL LUGGAGE ONLINE
Visit us at *www.llbean.com/traveler*

SHOP THE L.L. BEAN CATALOG
Call us any time of the day or night to place an order or request our TRAVELER'S catalog. 1-800-221-4221.

ORDER BY FAX
United States 1-207-552-3080. Canada and International 1-207-552-4080.

VISIT OUR RETAIL AND FACTORY STORES
Our retail stores are located in Freeport, Maine and Tysons Corner, Virginia. Shop our factory stores in Maine, New Hampshire, Delaware, Virginia and Oregon.

FAST FEDEX® DELIVERY
We ship most orders by fast, reliable FedEx delivery within 24 hours. Most customers receive their orders in two to three business days.

▶ Garment Bags

Garment bags are luggage for grown-ups: your clothes have to be tall before you need a suitcase that folds over in half. Pullmans can carry full-length suits, too, but garment bags do a better job, and most have many useful features that you don't find in that flimsy bag you get when you buy a new suit or a formal gown at a department store. Adored by business travelers, garment bags are also useful if you're going on a cruise or heading for an out-of-town wedding or anywhere else that requires clothing that needs special attention.

CARRY-ON ARMOIRES If you use a garment bag, you can pack straight from your closet, then unpack simply by unfolding the bag and hanging it in the closet in your hotel. Because of the bag's shape, your clothing can be folded fewer times, reducing the possibility of wrinkles.

LOOKING AT GARMENT BAGS

When shopping, compare the interiors of several bags. Consider whether the space allocation makes sense to you. Would you prefer to have fewer restrictions? Also spend some time experimenting in the store to see which size works best. Garment bags come in several different lengths, the longest up to 56 inches. This may not be an issue for men who are packing only suits, but for a woman, a short bag means that the hems of longer dresses and coats must be folded back. A taller person should have no trouble carrying a 45-inch bag; someone of average height may feel more comfortable with one that measures 40 inches.

Polished, professional, and often lighter than pullmans, they're also ideal as carry-ons; you can either hang them

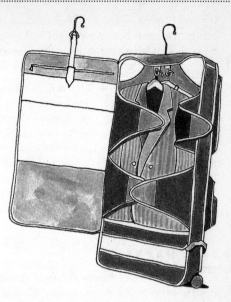

in the cabin closet or fold them over and place them in the overhead compartment. (Slim garment bags made of light nylon are particularly handy, especially for overnight business trips.)

As your main piece of luggage, you'll probably want a sturdy model made of a heavier fabric and roomy enough to hold enough clothes for a two-week trip. This kind of garment bag is generally longer, has inside and outside pockets for stowing other garments and accessories, and comes with locks. For ultimate flexibility, you may want to purchase both a lightweight garment bag and a heavy-duty one.

OPEN SESAME? Most bags open like books, but others have a flap that unzips and folds down to let you get at your clothing. Some variations on this theme are more successful than others. In a third design, where the flap opens on the diagonal, reaching everything can be tricky. Yet another style requires that you unzip horizontal zippers top and bottom as well as a perpendicular one down the center. This can be inconvenient and time-consuming. Some models have a handy fold-out accessories panel that can be detached and hung in the closet by itself.

VARIATIONS ON A THEME While some garment bags are bags pure and simple, others are divided into compartments to help you organize your things. Some have interior pockets of various sizes, often made of mesh so you can locate items quickly and easily. Although garment bags typically fold in half, some newer models fold in thirds, producing a smaller and more portable package. Some bags have wheels. One well-known manufacturer of adventure luggage sells a garment bag with zip-out backpack straps.

▶ Travel Packs

When the hordes of America's baby-boom generation first descended upon Europe in the late '60s and '70s, student visas and Eurailpasses in hand, they were called backpackers. They all carried lumpy Army-surplus packs with just enough room for a second pair of jeans, a couple of extra flowered shirts, and maybe (or maybe not) some underwear. These packs were ideal hippie gear, easy to sling into the back seat of someone else's car or to use for a pillow if you were sleeping in a train station overnight. But the Aussies and Germans who were going the same route had something still better; their packs were made of waterproof nylon and had hollow aluminum frames. Americans were quick to switch to these lighter packs and have been using them ever since. But like most other toys of the baby-boom generation they've been upscaled, upsized and downsized, and high-teched in every way imaginable by smart manufacturers who know a good market when they see one.

The new travel packs, a.k.a. backpacks, simply can't be beat for rugged vacations—rugged being trips that have you hauling your belongings for miles at a time, through swampland or down the endless streets of the urban jun-

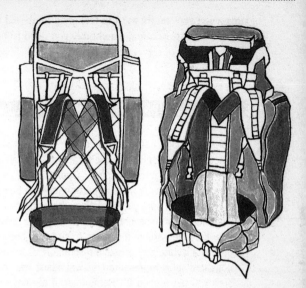

gle. Packs are great for casual vacation clothing, and they project an air of romantic independence—getting one is kind of like opting for a Harley-Davidson over a mini-van. But like mini-vans, they're forgiving when you want to stuff in just one more thing. They leave your hands free so that you can hold a map, take notes, or help a child. And while they're generally lighter than some other kinds of suitcases, many have a strategically placed handle that lets you pack and carry them like a pullman. Packs are also a good family solution—get them for your youngsters so that they may carry their own gear.

SIZE Like duffel bags, packs are measured in cubic inches. There's a 3,200-cubic-inch carry-on size, and for more serious treks you can opt for a capacity of 5,100 or 6,000 cubic inches.

STRUCTURE Not all packs are equal. Some have an exterior frame of lightweight aluminum. These are really best for mountain climbers and campers. Others have a very flexible internal frame, which makes them perfect for trips when you simply want to feel unencumbered by luggage. Yet before you make a choice, you need to be clear about the type of travel you're planning.

LL BEAN'S TIPS FOR SHOPPING FOR A PACK

For backpacks, head to the nearest L.L.Bean store. Once there, imagine yourself packing. Can you fit what you need into the space? Open several packs. Do you like the way the compartments have been divided? Are you sure you're getting what you want? Be persistent: Try on several packs, to get a true sense of how they feel. Adjust the straps to suit your body size and to alleviate any possible discomfort. Our knowledgeable sales representatives will assist you to ensure you get a good fit. Remember, if the pack isn't comfortable empty, it's going to make you miserable when it's full. L.L.Bean also makes it easy—and safe—to shop online. Visit *www.llbean.com* to browse our full range of travel and adventure packs.

WHAT'S COOL Some packs are designed specifically for women, taking into account their smaller size in the placement and adjustability of the straps. Convertibility is another definite plus in a travel pack; a zippered panel can hide back and waist straps to magically transform packs into more traditional-looking luggage. While most packs have a large central compartment and outside pockets, some also have extra removable pouches. Many packs also come with a removable day pack; when attached it functions as a pocket, but unzip it and—voilà!—it's a separate bag that you can carry around for an afternoon of sightseeing or a morning on the trails. Some packs have an expandable main compartment that zips open to provide extra room for souvenirs or some cheese and a loaf of bread.

▶ Laptop Luggage

With the advent of notebook computers, doing your work while you fly is as simple as can be. Some aircraft are even equipped with modem ports so you can go on-line in mid-flight.

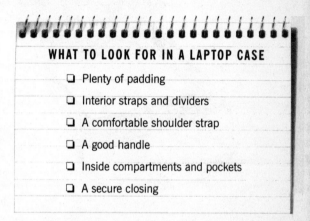

WHAT TO LOOK FOR IN A LAPTOP CASE

❑ Plenty of padding

❑ Interior straps and dividers

❑ A comfortable shoulder strap

❑ A good handle

❑ Inside compartments and pockets

❑ A secure closing

You're better off looking for a case for your laptop in a computer store. Your choices are generally supple black leather or black canvas, both of which go with anything. When buying a computer carry-on case, look for a light frame and plenty of protective padding as well as a shoulder strap and a briefcase-style handle that are securely attached. Inside there should be straps and movable dividers to keep your computer snugly positioned in transit, as well as compartments for your portable printer, docking station, transformers, and spare hard drives, and easy-to-access pockets to hold disks, books, papers, and pens. The closing should be secure—perhaps a sturdy zipper. Most computer carry-ons are essentially only modified attaché cases, but a few manufacturers offer backpack-style models with a pair of adjustable shoulder straps. These are great if you plan to bicycle or hike and want to take your computer along, though they don't have the boxy shape that conforms so snugly to the computer.

AVOID AIRPORT SCAMS

When carrying your computer through airport security checkpoints, you'll have to lay it down on the X-ray belt to be scanned: Although some computer experts warn that repeated scans may damage the hard drive, passengers rarely have a choice. Tip #1: Don't let anyone distract you once your computer has started moving on that belt. Move promptly through the body check and be ready to pick up your computer as soon as it emerges from the scanner. Airport thieves, working in pairs, know this is a ripe opportunity for lifting laptops. Don't be their next victim. Tip #2: Keep your laptop charged so that you can turn it on if you're asked to do so, to prove that it is what it seems to be.

To Wheel or Not to Wheel?

No wonder the invention of the wheel was such a watershed event in human civilization: Everything we've slapped a wheel onto has become an instant success (look at in-line skates, IV poles, etc.) When you think about it, it was only a matter of time before wheels sprouted out of suitcases and changed the nature of modern luggage. Perhaps it can all be traced back to the bellhop's dolly. Or perhaps this great flash of inspiration occurred when someone noticed the speed and dexterity with which flight attendants were able to race through the airport, gracefully pulling their baggage behind them on strap-on dollies. In any case, the innovation arrived just in time. With our peripatetic lifestyles, we need luggage that can keep up with us. Wheels certainly do the trick, and so it's not surprising that wheeled suitcases have taken over in luggage stores and luggage departments all across America.

Poor Robert could have used one on his business trip to Italy, when he packed his clothing in three small duffels and several shopping bags. In his own words, his Oxford-cloth shirts wound up looking like "pressed flowers." A large suitcase with wheels would have been a better solution—even though it might have been heavier than his collection of small bags, it would have been far more maneuverable, as he'd only have needed one hand to manage it.

Although you can find duffels with wheels and travel packs with wheels, most suitcases with wheels come in a classic pullman shape turned on end—sometimes known as vertical pullmans—with a variety of interior fittings; you pull them by either a strap or a built-in telescoping handle. Large ones hold as much as a standard suitcase, and smaller ones can be wheeled aboard as carry-ons. If you're traveling with a family, you may choose to bring everybody's stuff in one big suitcase—in which case you'll definitely want it to have wheels.

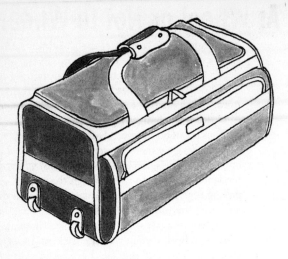

Some suitcases with wheels are advertised as cases and luggage carts in one; you simply place your computer case, briefcase, or smaller suitcase on the extended handle. Easily handled as they are, they show you to be in control of your luggage, and if you're on a business trip, that's a good impression to make.

Once you've narrowed your selection to several bags, take each one for a walk. Do you feel pressure on your back when you pull it? Is the handle at the right height, so that you don't have to crouch like a caveman dragging his club? Is most of the weight of the case balanced on the wheels, or are you carrying much of it yourself? Does the handle feel good in your hand? Increase your speed—does the bag begin to wobble? Stop suddenly—what happens?

Are You a Carry-On Traveler?

Savvy globetrotters have always known how to travel with less. My sexagenarian friend George is a good example. Possibly one of the earliest carry-on customers, George travels for months at a time with one of those small shoulder-strap cabin bags the airlines used to give away as perks. In it he packs several T-shirts, one or two pairs of trousers and shorts, and some underwear. Every night he does a little laundry. George's wash-and-go crew cut barely requires a comb. Forced to economize on luggage because he uses crutches to get around, he's found that packing light actually enables him to travel on his own terms. And oh, the places he goes!

Am I advocating that we all live out of cabin bags? Absolutely not. There are going to be times when you'll want, or need, to have a bit more with you. If you're in the fashion or design business, in which wearing the same pair of shoes three nights in a row is right up there with mixing stripes and polka dots, you'll want to take a more extensive wardrobe. Cruise vacations, at least on larger ships, are another time to pack more lavishly—your luggage remains on board for the entire voyage, and that extra evening dress or dinner jacket will help you enjoy deluxe shipboard life to the hilt. (After you've checked out the handy packing lists in Chapter 3, however, even you may be able to cut your heft in half.)

PART TECHNIQUE, PART TRAVEL PHILOSOPHY

There is something important to be learned by studying George's approach to travel—he simply won't let his gear get him down. Streamlining your packing means that you are in control of your luggage instead of at its mercy. (Think of a dog leading its master and then look around the next time you go to an airport: You'll definitely see people being led by their bags.) Traveling with nothing but carry-on luggage promotes self-reliance. It leaves you free from the weight of things you really don't need. When you land in a strange place and there isn't so much

RATIONALIZATIONS OF AN OVERPACKER

For some people, checking luggage is simply part of the trip—they are willing to put up with the hassle because they will be happier in the end. But are they, really?

"YOU NEVER KNOW WHAT YOU'RE GOING TO NEED" We've all heard this before, and many of us have said it ourselves. But times have changed. On our swiftly shrinking planet, camera film is now for sale in Kenyan villages. These days, if you haven't brought enough of something—or, heaven forfend, forgotten a crucial item—chances are you'll be able to find it wherever you're going. Often, this can lead to pleasant discoveries. My friend Bruce likes to shop for toiletries abroad—that's how he discovered he prefers English shaving cream over American brands. Another friend of mine, Jon, began a lifelong love affair with honey soap in Nice, while Gregg makes a point of buying deodorant in each country he visits. He sees it as the first order of business in a new place—it lends a kind of wacky mission to his sightseeing.

"I WON'T HAVE ENOUGH DRESSY CLOTHING" The citizens of the world have all relaxed a lot over the last 20 years or so, with us jeaned-and-sneakered Americans leading the way. So why does an American going abroad feel the need to pull out all the stops? (If you've ever been to the London theater, you'll have noticed that all the dressed-up folks in tuxedos and furs in the front rows are package-tour Americans; the Brits themselves are in jeans and sweaters, up in the balcony.)

Remember that you're a tourist; you're going to look, sound, and smell like a tourist no matter what you do. So you may as well be comfortable. Today, an understated ensemble in a dark color can take you everywhere. Black is always appropriate for evening, and it can be dressed up or down. A dark suit for men, or a simple jacket and tie, can do wonders.

"I'M NOT BUYING A THING" Let's be honest here: Chances are, you're going to buy a lot of things. And it's a safe bet that you'll want to wear what you buy even though you've packed more than enough to wear. Savvy travelers pack with these simple truisms in mind. Some even take along old clothing, buy new clothing, and leave their old duds in the hotel as a kind of reverse souvenir.

"THE BLUE FOR MONDAY, THE RED FOR TUESDAY..." Instead of packing extra outfits, fill in with accessories such as scarves, ties, and shirts. Accessories take up very little room and can dramatically change the personality of a basic outfit.

"JUST A FEW COMFORTS OF HOME..." Travelers who are daunted by leaving the familiar behind tend to overpack. If you're among them, you need to pack a sense of adventure! Edna St. Vincent Millay once wrote, "There isn't a train I wouldn't take, no matter where it's going." Obviously a carry-on packer. Remember, no matter how much you try, you can't take it all with you.

as a Handi-Cart to greet you, it's nice to know you can manage on your own. Less physical baggage can often mean less emotional baggage, as well; in today's complicated world there's an exhilarating feeling of freedom and lightness that comes from living out of just one bag.

Business travelers appreciate the time carry-on luggage saves at both ends of their trip—no long waits at the baggage carousel, no possibility of the luggage being lost or damaged by the airline. Once they've discovered the freedom of traveling with carry-on luggage only, they often prefer to pack that way for personal vacations as well.

Because most airlines allow two carry-ons (and that's in addition to a purse, a camera bag, and a diaper bag), you really can bring enough gear for a two-week trip if you pack super-efficiently—and skip the baggage carousel scene entirely.

EVEN PACK RATS NEED A CARRY-ON A proper carry-on bag should be a carefully considered part of everyone's luggage wardrobe. Even if you do check most of your belongings, you'll probably want to bring some things into the cabin with you—valuables, a camera, reading material for the flight, your toiletry kit, and toys and snacks if you're traveling with children. (Look around you on your next trip. You'll be surprised how many people, even those with a mountain of matching luggage, stuff their on-board items into any old bag they can find.) And remember that when you've reached your destination, you may still need a small bag to carry around when you attend meetings or see the sights. Maps, travel guides, cameras, passports, phrase books—they do add up. Get a carry-on that can double as a daily tote bag and you've got it made.

In a way, carry-ons are not a separate category of luggage at all, but a subset of the others: there are carry-on garment bags, carry-on duffels, carry-on travel packs, even carry-on suitcases with wheels. To these can be added a fifth type, the carry-on tote, which can be opened at the top to allow easy access to your stuff. The defining element is size.

Carry-on luggage works well for both business and pleasure trips. A 22-inch suitcase with wheels with a suiter compartment is perfect for formal business trips, as are lightweight garment bags designed to carry suits, dresses, and formal wear with a minimum of wrinkling. Garment bags don't fit under the seat, but they can be stowed either in the overhead compartment or in the front of the cabin. For vacation travelers, mid-size duffels and travel packs also function well as carry-ons, fitting either under the seat or overhead.

In the store, check out the same details you would on a full-sized pullman, garment bag, duffel, or travel pack. Then practice carrying several different styles. Consider how you prefer to tote a bag. Are you most comfortable rolling it, slinging it over your shoulder, or holding it by a handle? If a bag offers more than one carrying option, all the better.

HOW BIG CAN YOU GO? The main plane require-
ment is that a bag be small enough to fit either in the overhead bin or under the seat in front of you. The dimensions
should total 45 inches: 20 x 16 x 9, for example, or 21 x 13
x 8, or 22 x 14 x 9. Although the space at your feet is not as
large, remember that it's yours and no one else's; the space
over your head may be a different matter. With so many
travelers opting for carry-ons these days, snagging compartment space on a sold-out flight is not for the faint of heart.
Make your primary carry-on one that fits under the seat.

And remember that airport terminals can go on for miles,
and also that you may be using this bag as your daily tote.
A carry-on has to be easy to carry on, or it doesn't deserve
the name.

HELP FOR OVERPACKERS Whether you're trying
to cram in everything for your trip or just using your carry-
on to take care of overflow from your other luggage, ex-
pandability is a plus. Soft-sided bags generally function
best in the carry-on realm, so if you've opted for hard-
sided in the rest of your luggage, shop around for something soft-sided that coordinates decently with the rest of
your bags instead of a matching carry-on.

Note that while a light frame can be helpful in protecting your belongings—especially in a garment bag—it's a
good idea to avoid anything too heavy to carry or too rigid
to fit into the spaces provided on aircraft.

Consider how and what you'll be packing into your carry-
on, and how many different compartments you'll want. If
you intend to carry all your trip gear in your carry-on,
you'll need a bag that can tidily store clothes as well as
toiletries and reading material. It's also a good idea to
have some outside pockets to hold items you may want to
get at mid-flight.

THE GORILLA TEST You may think that a carry-on
needn't be as durable as your other bags, since you'll always be the one handling it. But what happens when your

fellow passengers start "rearranging" the overhead compartment? When the flight attendant "assists" you by shoving your overstuffed duffel farther under the seat in front of you? Or when you're asked to check your carry-on—the airline's prerogative? You'll still want a fabric that will hold up well, either a supple leather or a sturdy nylon or canvas (remember the importance of portability).

Zippers and clasps should be as sturdy as on other types of luggage. While locks may not be as critical, remember that even if you never check this bag, you may have to leave it unattended in a hotel baggage room or elsewhere at your destination.

How to Judge Quality

The first trip I took with my sporty new garment bag was a long weekend to the French province of Burgundy. At the baggage carousel after landing back in New York, I was horrified to see what approached: my poor little bag had a mangled shoulder strap. When I bent to slip the strap over my shoulder, the part attached to the garment bag tore right off. I was crestfallen, but continued to use the bag for several more years. (Oh, all right, I'm still using it.) During a trip a few years ago, I met a man traveling with the same garment bag, also sans shoulder strap. Apparently, his, too, had given up the ghost early on. Does anyone see a structural flaw here?

The point is that not all bags are created equal. Luggage varies tremendously. Although people who travel only occasionally may not need the same level of durability as those who check their luggage many times each month, even seldom-used luggage takes a beating—and nobody wants to retrieve a shredded bag on the baggage carousel or have a suitcase fall apart mid-trip. In any case, you should know what you're getting for the money you're spending. And don't pay top dollar for bottom-of-the-barrel quality.

So carefully compare luggage from different manufacturers and even different pieces within a single line. Open the bag in the store and look closely at how it's made.

HOW'S THE FRAME? Fiberglass inner structures (frames) ensure both light weight and strength. Inner structures may also be made of aluminum, wood, durable molded plastic compounds, or any combination of the above. A weighty frame will make a case heavy even before it's packed. Frame materials are often listed on the luggage tag; your friendly neighborhood luggage salesperson should also be able to tell you what they are.

FEATURES TO INSPECT

- ❏ Color
- ❏ Construction
- ❏ Fabric
- ❏ Frame
- ❏ Handles

- ❏ Hardware
- ❏ Straps
- ❏ Waterproofing
- ❏ Webbing
- ❏ Wheels

IS THE CONSTRUCTION GOOD? On cases with zippers, look for taped seams, in which a strip of cloth reinforces the zipper and bag connection; this prevents fraying. On the outside of the bag, joints should be covered with either leather or nylon piping or welts to reinforce the seams and absorb wear and tear. Also, seams should be lockstitched, a method in which each stitch is reinforced, or locked, to stay in place and stand alone. (Look for the loop around each individual stitch.) This way, if one stitch happens to break, it won't take the next one with it and unravel your seam.

WILL THE FABRIC HOLD UP? Fabric counts for a lot in luggage. Leather luggage—long a status symbol, no matter whose initials it's embossed with—can be very durable and looks marvelous (until it gets scuffed, that is), but it is often too heavy to be carried even when it's empty. Top-grain or full-grain leather, the outermost layer of the hide, is stronger and more durable than leather made from splits, the layers of hide that are split off from underneath the top grain. Luggage made from splits costs less but is more likely to show wear.

Among the various fabrics available, those that are heavier protect the bag's contents better and stand up to sharp objects that might cause tears or rips in transit. Popular these days are ballistic nylon and Cordura nylon. Ballistic nylon is a bit more expensive but worth it. The same bag made of Cordura or Cordura Plus costs less and is still pretty sturdy. Although tweed and brocade bags may appear sturdier than nylon ones, they are slashable and the thicker fabric adds weight.

Among luggage connoisseurs, the denier, or thickness, of the yarn used in the fabric is a major issue. The higher the denier, the stronger the yarn and the fabric woven from it. Unfortunately, it's difficult to compare denier from bag to bag. Some manufacturers do not list it on their informational tags, and even luggage salespeople are often unable to determine what it might be. The important thing to keep in mind is that few bags on the market are made of fabric woven from less than 400-denier yarn; many fabric yarns are between 400- and 1,000-denier, and a few are as high as 2,000-denier. If your bag pleases you in all other ways, don't sweat the denier.

There are some other unusual fabrics that are perfect for the traveler concerned about the environment. These include Fortrel EcoSpun, a durable material made from recycled plastic bottles, and fabric woven from hemp.

Choose fabric in a color that you like and that harmonizes with any other luggage you own. Keep in mind that lighter colors show stains faster, whereas darker colors are more likely to show dust.

MONSOON-PROOF? Whether you're trapped in an Indian monsoon or a steady Seattle downpour, or you've got your luggage on a cartop carrier the day the hurricane blows through, waterproof luggage comes in handy. Poor Caragh had an incident in which her black canvas bag was drenched. When she unpacked, she discovered that all her light-colored clothing had been dyed to match the bag. How to avoid this? The best all-around fabric would be a Cordura or ballistic nylon with a waterproof seal—most bags are not waterproofed on the outside, but treated on the inside with a moisture-resisting sealant. Check the informational tag on the luggage or ask the salesperson to explain how the bag has been waterproofed. If you require special protection from water for camping, rafting, or some other adventure expedition, buy at a store that specializes in more rugged gear; the salespeople at places like this can often discuss the relative merits of manufacturers and their luggage from their own personal experience on trips like the one you're planning.

LOOK AT THE CLOSINGS The simpler, the better. If there's a zipper, it should be tough and run smoothly. Zippers should also be double-stitched (stitched on both sides of the zipper) and self-repairing or large, very sturdy, and smooth-running. Zippers made of polyester coils that have been woven or sewn to tapes can take a lot of pressure and can be healed if they pop open. Large zipper pulls are always easier to work with.

GET LOCKS You should also be able to lock your bag. Small combination locks, which are designed for luggage, may come on hard-sided pullmans and are a plus if you tend to lose keys. The more rivets or screws that attach it to the case, the more secure the lock will be.

Luggage that closes with two-way zippers may come with small locks designed to hook through the zipper pulls on each compartment.

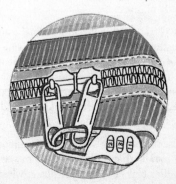

TEENY TINY ZIPPER PULLS? NO LOCKS?

TIP

If the pulls on your suitcase are small, attach large paper clips to them so you can get a better grip. If your bag doesn't have locks, it's a good idea to buy some. The most secure of these are combination locks. And if you haven't had a chance to buy locks or have forgotten them, try "locking" the zippers with a large safety pin; even the smallest barrier is sometimes enough to stop a thief who's short on time. If your luggage comes with keys, put them on your key chain so they don't get lost.

GET A GRIP ON THE HANDLES Handle construction may well be the most overlooked detail, and yet it is crucial—whatever the style of luggage. Be sure to pick up the suitcase, and make sure that it's comfortable in your hand; any slight discomfort will be magnified when it's fully loaded.

On a pullman, and on garment bags (at the fold), look to see whether the handle is attached to the bag with screws or with rivets. (A handle attached with screws can be replaced; when a riveted handle comes off, it's down for the count.) Also note whether the handle is padded on the underside, and whether it's covered with leather or only sturdy plastic.

For vertical pullmans and duffels, count how many handles there are on the bag: Is there one on the side as well as on the top? Side handles are a great help when you're lifting the bag onto a closet shelf or into an overhead compartment on a plane. On travel packs, in addition to the back straps, there should be handles on at least two sides of the bag.

Most suitcases with wheels are equipped with a telescoping handle that pulls out of the case when needed. Some handles can be locked in place, whereas others remain free to slide in and out at random (and if they can, they will—choose one that locks). The handle system should be well-protected, whether it's housed inside the bag or outside. (Not all handles measure up, however. Be sure the handle is sturdy, especially if you plan to hang a briefcase or tote bag over it). Pull the handle out and tilt the bag; watch to see whether it stays rigid—if it bends at all it is probably too weak to take any more weight.

CHECK THE STRAPS AND WEBBING Shoulder straps for duffels and garment bags should be made of wide webbing, and ideally they should be padded where they rest on your shoulders. Note how the webbing is attached to the bag: is it reinforced with box and cross stitching? Choose a duffel with a shoulder strap in addition to two center handles—this increases your carrying options for times when you'll need your hands free. When shopping around, ignore the salesperson's nasty looks and spend some time adjusting the straps and handles to suit your size—if the duffel doesn't hang well from your shoulder, or seems unwieldy when held by its handle, you'll want to know now, not the day of the trip.

On pullmans, notice where the handles are placed. It is helpful to have both side and top handles, for easier portability.

It's equally important for the straps of travel packs to be padded, as they will be resting on your shoulders for long periods of time. Look for a padded waist or hip strap as well, to steady and center the bag on your body. All straps should be adjustable for height and weight.

TEST THE WHEELS If the wheels don't work on a piece of wheeled luggage, you might as well have bought a regular pullman. Four wheels make a suitcase more stable and easier to roll than do two wheels (think car vs. motorcycle). The wheels should also be spaced as widely apart as possible and at least slightly recessed into the bag's frame so that it provides some protection for them— an exposed wheel can be neatly severed from your bag by a pothole, an uneven cobblestone, or a seemingly innocuous curb. One manufacturer uses large, sturdy in-line skate wheels for the ultimate in rollability and performance. Insist on smooth-rolling wheels that are firmly bolted in place.

INSPECT THE HARDWARE In garment bags, pay special attention to the brackets that hold the clothes hangers in place. Some bags come with two brackets, which allows you to form alternative layers of clothing and cuts down on wrinkles. The hook that you'll hang the bag from should be well secured when not in use: Does it retract into the bag, snap tight to the bag, or dangle uselessly and dangerously? Is the hook itself strong or flimsy? Remember that it must bear the weight of the entire bag when hung in a closet. Also consider the clothes hangers. Are there enough of them? Or can you use your own? It's handiest if you can move your garments straight from your closet into the bag, without having to switch hangers.

WHAT'S INSIDE? Are there straps to hold clothing in place? In garment bags, look for models that have two straps that crisscross over the top half of the clothing as well as a center strap—these really do keep your things from sliding around and wrinkling.

2

PRIME PACKING PRINCIPLES

I once traveled with a bright, creative man who was, alas, somewhat disorganized. For a week's business trip in the Caribbean—which we were told in advance would involve island hopping in tiny planes—he packed three large duffel bags, each of them half empty. Since we were traveling to a warm-weather destination, I couldn't figure out what was in those bags. Neither could anyone else on the trip. But it all became frighteningly clear at the airport, as he unzipped a duffel so he could locate his missing airplane ticket. Inside, he had a family-size box of tissues, magazines and books, swim trunks, a large beach towel, 10 or 12 compact disks, and a full-size shampoo bottle. A patina of baby powder covered everything—everything except the airplane ticket, which was nowhere to be found. Stuffed in among the balled-up shirts, shorts, and slacks in the next duffel were three pairs of shoes, a full-size iron, and a canister of tennis balls. Still no ticket. On to the third duffel, which contained cameras, film, recording equipment, miscellaneous papers—and the airplane ticket. When he began to search for his passport, I had to turn away; I knew my limits. I was dying to give him a packing lesson he'd never forget.

No matter how often we pack, certain dilemmas remain evergreen: How much to take without taking too much? How to fit it all in without causing excessive wrinkles? How to remember crucial items? Having a plan is a big help. Don't have one? Don't worry. By the end of this chapter, you'll have formulated an organized packing strategy even General Schwarzkopf would envy.

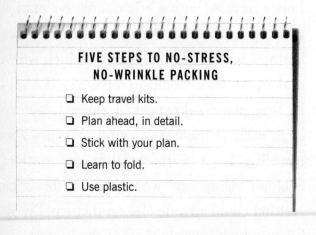

FIVE STEPS TO NO-STRESS, NO-WRINKLE PACKING

❏ Keep travel kits.

❏ Plan ahead, in detail.

❏ Stick with your plan.

❏ Learn to fold.

❏ Use plastic.

The Advance Planning

Packing is like most enterprises in life: The better the plan going in, the more successful the venture will be. (Witness: Desert Storm as opposed to Vietnam, *Star Wars* as opposed to *Water World*, etc.)

The plan I recommend calls for different tasks to be completed over a period of time, so that much of the last-minute packing pressure is relieved. This is a very optimistic view of the world, in which you'll have months of happy anticipation before your much-awaited trip. In reality, you'll probably be told on Friday afternoon that you're expected Sunday morning for a week of meetings in Paris, and will spend the next 24 hours frantically throwing things into a valise. In a 1997 Fodor's Travel poll, 42.5% of the respondents confessed that they usually pack the day before or a few hours before they leave on a trip—and no doubt many of them had no one else to blame for this but their own procrastinating selves.

Still, there's a world of difference between hysterically flinging things into a suitcase and swiftly but thoughtfully assembling your gear. One key element is to have a series of travel kits always packed and at the ready (*see* Make a Travel Kit, *below*). Given that head start, an efficient packer can carry out the following plan in a leisurely month or a single disciplined day (showing grace under pressure, of course). My aim is to get you to thinking about the process of packing, and to see how a little planning during quiet times can save you in a crunch.

▶ Lay the Groundwork

The moment it looks as if you're really going to be taking a trip—perhaps the day you've finally booked the tickets or notified your office about when you'll be gone—begin to draw up a casual itinerary, a plan of what your days and evenings will be like as you travel. Is this a business trip on which you'll dress to impress at day-long meetings and seminars? A family vacation during which you and your children may be kneeling in the grass to make rubbings of gravestones? A honeymoon someplace where you and your love will wear nothing more than matching sarongs? Will you be staying in one place, or visiting several? Seeing the same people for the duration, or meeting new ones every few days? Each experience calls for a different wardrobe. Knowing what you will be doing means you can begin to plan what you'll be wearing, and that is the first step in the packing process.

Look into local customs as you plan. In some resort areas, an anything-goes dress code applies, while in others many restaurants frown on diners with bare feet or those wearing shorts, bathing suits, even T-shirts. Going abroad? Various countries maintain traditions of dress that differ from ours. In the Middle East, for example, women need to dress modestly—no miniskirts, no trousers. Anticipate such customs when planning your wardrobe. Before you go, check with the country's tourist office or consult a good guidebook.

PLAN YOUR WARDROBE, MAKE A LIST

Although 42.5% of the respondents to that Fodor's survey are last-minute packers, the next largest group—29%, nearly one-third of those surveyed—declare that they make lists and pack at least one week before a trip. Somehow even a mental list is never quite as effective as an actual list written on a piece of paper. Think about everything you'll need to take, from travel kits to incidentals to electrical items, and write everything down.

Look at your itinerary and note possible outfits next to each activity or meeting, including shoes and accessories. When I am preparing for a business trip as a travel journalist, my list might read as follows: Breakfast and six hotel site inspections—yellow sundress, sun hat, brown sandals, silver earrings. Rafting down the Martha Brae River—pink bathing suit, orange T-shirt, khaki shorts, sneakers, sunglasses. In this way, you'll become aware of your clothing needs and begin to form a tentative travel wardrobe.

TO PACK OR NOT TO PACK: DISPOSABLE DIAPERS

If your little one is still in diapers, one question looms large: Do you bring a whole trip's supply of disposable diapers or buy them when you get there?

Buying diapers shouldn't be a problem in the United States, although if you're arriving late in the day, you'll need enough to last until morning—the last thing you want to do on arrival is peel around town looking for Pampers. If you're heading for a resort, however, it may be hard to get off-site, and the resort shops won't necessarily sell diapers, or diapers in the size you need or at a price you consider acceptable to pay. (One mother recalls forking over $1.25 per diaper at a California resort.) If you're leaving the U.S., bringing your own diapers isn't such a bad idea. In the Caribbean, disposable diapers are very expensive; in Europe, prices aren't bad, but stores may stock only local brands, which aren't nearly as absorbent as the ones you're used to.

It all depends on the length of your trip. For a short beach vacation, take diapers (and invest in a washable swim diaper to cut down on the number of disposables you'll need). For a two-week jaunt to Europe, here's a compromise: take enough diapers to get through the first week, which buys you some time before you have to go diaper-hunting. If on Day Two you happen into a supermercado that sells Les Pampers at a decent price, all the better.

This is one situation where it is better to err on the side of packing more. After all, diapers don't weigh much, and though they consume a lot of suitcase room, on the other hand that's space that will be freed up by the return journey. And hey, you're traveling with small kids—the concept of packing light probably went out the window a long time ago.

CHECK IT TWICE Now make a new list, noting only the clothing you've chosen. Study it carefully. Notice how many times you've listed a specific item—shorts, for instance, or T-shirts—and also consider the colors of the clothes. Do you have shorts listed seven times for your seven-day trip? In that case, you'll probably be able to make do with only two or three pairs. Have you listed your lime-green Manolo Blahnik pumps just once? Better to leave them at home in favor of a more versatile pair of shoes.

It's also helpful to see how many outfits you can make with each article of clothing. A pair of black trousers, for example, can be dressed up or down; a navy or olive-green blazer looks great over jeans as well as business slacks. As a rule, women find that separates work far better than dresses, although dresses are necessary for certain occasions. Here, right here, is where your clothing editing begins, when you can consider all the variables calmly. It certainly beats gazing, panic-stricken, into the yawning mouth of your suitcase the evening before your 7 AM flight.

Try to coordinate your wardrobe around just two or three complimentary colors—black, gray, and red; navy, red, and white; brown, olive-green, and cream, etc. Doing this increases your outfit choices because everything goes with everything else, and you'll get more mileage out of fewer accessories. Don't pair black with navy on the same trip—each requires its own accessories, and they are not interchangeable.

Once you've pared down your list, choose a travel outfit for yourself, composed of items already noted. It may be a good idea to opt for the heaviest clothes on your list—wearing these items means you'll automatically have less to pack. If traveling casually, wear neat-looking, loose-fitting clothing. If you're a man traveling directly from the airport to a business meeting, you may want to wear a dress shirt, suit jacket, and comfortable pants, bringing your suit pants and a tie in a carry-on bag so that you can change just before or after landing. Women may wish to do the same, switching at journey's end from slacks into a skirt or dress pants and pumps.

ACCESSORIES—LESS IS MORE

When it comes to jewelry, remember the old adage: Less is more. When you're traveling, wearing a lot of flashy jewelry (even costume jewelry) can be as good as posting a neon sign over your head that reads: ROB ME. Besides, the more you take with you, the greater your chance of mislaying something by accident. (Never remove your jewelry, even when sleeping—to take off is to risk leaving behind.) So don't take what you don't want to lose—choose a few simple jewelry pieces that blend with everything and that you can wear all together without looking like Mr. T. You can always accessorize with scarves instead. If you must bring more jewelry than you can wear all at once, pack it on your person or in your carry-on bag.

GOING ABROAD? Check to see that you (and your traveling companions) have valid passports—that is, passports that will still be valid the month after you expect to return. Also make sure you have obtained any necessary visas. To apply for or renew a passport by mail, it's important to leave yourself some time: about four to five weeks for a new one, three to four weeks to renew one. If it's an emergency situation and you simply don't have that much time, you can apply in person at a U.S. Passport Office, and they will do their best to expedite your request for an additional fee. To all you procrastinators out there: Believe me when I tell you that you should take care of your passport in advance by mail. Doing it in person is painfully time-consuming. (Note that, for a fee, various businesses—check the Yellow Pages—will happily arrange for someone to do any necessary in-person waiting for you. They can get you a passport quickly—often within a day if your circumstances require it.) For more information about obtaining or renewing passports in the United States, contact the Office of Passport Services (tel. 202/647–0518).

Also check a guidebook or call the Centers for Disease Control Prevention Hotline (tel. 404/332–4555) to get information about any inoculations required in your destination. Then consult your physician. Do this early: Some shots must be administered over a period of weeks, while others take time to become active.

If you're traveling to countries where health advisories apply, speak with your doctor about malaria pills or other preventive medicine.

HEADING SOUTH THIS WINTER?

When it's cold at home and you're flying to a warm destination, leave your heavy coat behind; you may be able to lock it in your car's trunk if leaving your car at the airport, or rent an airport travel locker. To get through the short time you'll be spending in the cold without the customary overcoat, wear extra layers of the clothing you're bringing along. Do wear a hat, scarf, and gloves—items that take up little room once you've reached your balmy destination.

▶ Get Busy and Get It Done

Now that you've laid the groundwork for your packing, it's time to start implementing your plans.

WORK ON YOUR WARDROBE Now that you've assembled a tentative wardrobe, go through the clothes themselves and decide what will need to be washed, dry-cleaned, hemmed—and get it done.

If you're traveling with children, have the youngsters try on their vacation clothing in advance—they will probably have outgrown some of it since the last time they wore it.

CALL YOUR HOTEL Inquire about laundry services, in-room hair dryers, irons, ironing boards, cribs, high chairs, complimentary toiletries, and other amenities. Knowing you can leave some or all of these items at home will help you pare down your packing list and make your suitcase a bit lighter.

GO SHOPPING Does your wardrobe plan require a comfortable pair of oxford-style shoes that will take you to the city sights by day and the theater at night? A dressy blouse that will turn your suit skirt into a dinner outfit? Buy them now. If your youngsters have outgrown key clothing items, don't wait until the night before the trip to replace them.

If you don't have a first-aid kit, buy yourself a small plastic-lined case and create one. Make sure you have enough of any prescription medication and/or vitamins you need to take—count out enough doses to last you for the length of your trip plus a few days beyond, in case you are unavoidably detained. Buy an electrical current converter and plug adapter if you need one. If your luggage is shot, read Chapter 1 and get busy!

TAKE CARE OF YOUR HOME This is also a good time to ask a kind neighbor or friend to keep an eye on your house or apartment, water your plants, and collect your newspapers and mail while you are gone. (Some people insist that it's preferable not to stop delivery altogether, lest it become apparent that you're not in residence.) Call the kennel to arrange for pet care.

IDENTIFY YOUR LUGGAGE Label it both inside and out, with your name and telephone number or your business card. If a thief gets a look at your home address, he's sure to head off on a little business trip of his own. Some airlines require that your tags bear an address—that's fine, just use your company's. If you work out of your home, be sure to include your firm name to make it look more like a business address.

The chances are good that other people own the exact same luggage you do—it's inevitable. What's not inevitable is their taking your bag home by accident. Mark your luggage to give it personality, something that transforms it from an old bag into an experienced valise. Even carry-on aficionados who don't know the business end of a baggage carousel will appreciate this tip, as it works just as well in a crowded hotel lobby, in front of a motor coach, wherever there's lots of luggage. While monograms are helpful, they might be too subtle for a tired passenger who's just come off the red-eye from L.A. I like to loop a bright orange bandanna around my suitcase handle, but you could use a ribbon, a garter belt, sausage links. . . Be creative, but also be careful: Displaying an "Undertakers do it in the deep-freeze" sticker might result in a rather solitary vacation.

FOLLOW THE WEATHER Start checking the temperatures for your destination in *The New York Times,* watch CNN International or the Weather Channel, or call 900/WEATHER or check the Web. Having up-to-date weather information allows you to pack appropriately and also to consider buying sunscreen, insect repellent, long johns, or whatever is needed for that particular climate. I'll never forget my two-month trip to London in January and February of 1987: Told that England's winter chill is really quite mild, I arrived clad in a thin raincoat to face some of the coldest, snowiest weather in British history. I don't think I need to remind you of the scarcity of central heating in London, at least in the late '80s. Had I checked the weather before leaving the States, I could have avoided paying most of my holiday bonus to Federal Express to deliver my winter coat and flannel sheets.

PACKING FOR TWO?

If you are traveling with a companion, get your dual acts together: One of you packs the iron, the other takes the hair dryer, and so forth.

TIP.

Make a Travel Kit

Preparing an assortment of travel kits filled with important travel items will save you packing time and aggravation in the long run. Because the kits will have been prepared far in advance, you'll be less likely to forget something. Chris and Nina, a couple I know who travel extensively for their jobs, routinely buy two of everything—makeup, toiletries, etc.—and keep one set permanently packed inside their luggage.

▶ A Toiletries Kit

From the Mickey Mouse–themed bottles and jars stocked at Walt Disney World properties to the lavish Lanvin toiletries found at chic Paris hotels, it seems that almost every kind of accommodation today has amenities in the bathroom—shampoo and conditioner, a sewing kit, a shoe polisher, body lotion, etc. Even economy hotels have joined in, placing small baskets filled with washcloths, tiny bars of Ivory soap, and plastic flowers by their stall showers. Handy as they may be, however, the kits tend to lack certain essentials: I have come across toothpaste in a hotel amenities kit exactly once, and I think it was left by a previous occupant. Travelers loyal to a particular brand will undoubtedly want to bring their own stuff, no matter how elegant the label of the freebies. So even if you call ahead to your hotel and verify that your bathroom contains an amenities basket, you'll still want to bring along some basic toiletries. The idea here is to select the smallest size of everything, keep it all in one convenient place, and guard against leakage.

These days, lots of personal-care products are available in small sizes—shaving cream, shampoo, conditioner, mouthwash, deodorant. Even name-brand cosmetics lines offer travel-size face creams and cleansers, often included in department store giveaways. (I know a man who won't go anywhere without his 12 different travel-size bottles of Kiehl's skin products. I mean anywhere—he takes them

WHAT'S IN YOUR TOILETRIES KIT

- ❑ Bath soap
- ❑ Bottle opener
- ❑ Cologne or perfume
- ❑ Comb and brush
- ❑ Spare contact lenses
- ❑ Contact-lens supplies
- ❑ Corkscrew
- ❑ Cotton swabs
- ❑ Dental floss
- ❑ Deodorant
- ❑ Eyeglass repair kit
- ❑ Facial cleanser
- ❑ First-aid kit
- ❑ Hair conditioner
- ❑ Hair dryer
- ❑ Hand lotion
- ❑ Insect repellent
- ❑ Laundry detergent
- ❑ Makeup
- ❑ Matches
- ❑ Moisturizer
- ❑ Mouthwash
- ❑ Nail clippers
- ❑ Nail file
- ❑ Nail polish, remover
- ❑ Razor
- ❑ Small screwdriver
- ❑ Sewing kit
- ❑ Shampoo
- ❑ Shaving cream
- ❑ Extra shoelaces
- ❑ Sink stopper
- ❑ Styling gel
- ❑ Sunscreen
- ❑ Swiss Army knife
- ❑ Tissues
- ❑ Toothbrush
- ❑ Toothpaste
- ❑ Tweezers
- ❑ Wipes

to the office, too.) Travel-size products save important packing space for crucial items available in full-size only, such as the one styling gel in the world that works on your hair. Buy travel-size products whenever you see them, so that you can replenish your stock as needed. Or buy small plastic bottles, then refill as needed from your full-size house-bound bottles. But don't fill them all the way up—

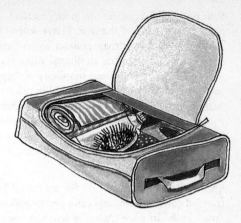

changes in air pressure during a flight can cause the contents to expand and leak out of the top.

Consider how to make each item easier or lighter to pack. Remove things like facial tissues from their bulky boxes; to keep them fresh, slip them into a resealable sandwich bags. Ditto for baby wipes—good for no-water hand washing (and stain removal, according to some travelers).

LAUNDRY, ANYONE? People seem to be sharply divided about doing laundry while away. Some insist they don't have the time, and willingly haul extra clothing to compensate, while others prefer to pack a little lighter and wash a few items in the sink each evening. No matter which side you're on, it's helpful to travel with a small bottle of detergent or Woolite (look for the travel-size packages of Woolite—they're wonderful). Even if you're not planning to wash, an errant stain may send you scurrying for the stuff, and you'll be glad you had it.

THINK SHORTCUTS Look for ways to make your daily habits more travel-friendly, too. After all, you are going away for a specific period of time. Women may wish to pack one all-purpose cream rather than individual hand, body, and face creams. Scented body cream is a good substitute for perfume. Cotton pads pre-moistened with nail polish remover are more practical, and safer to pack, than a bottle of the stuff. I have several friends who gladly leave at home their contact lenses (and six different solutions and electric sterilizers) when traveling, opting instead for the ease and simplicity of eyeglasses. Men may wish to shave with a disposable razor rather than dealing with the hassles—and weight—of their usual electric shaver plus a current converter. Use an electric toothbrush? Leave it at home and buy a person-powered model—again, you're saving space, weight, and converter hassles.

ESSENTIAL TOOLS As for my friend Pete, a well-traveled guy, the most important part of his kit is his Swiss Army knife. In mere inches of space, it equips him with scissors, a toothpick, a nail file, a bottle opener, a screwdriver, and a small knife. (Pete recommends that you buy the real McCoy, as other pocket knives are made from flimsy material and break easily.) But every Swiss Army knife has different components. If yours omits scissors, corkscrew, bottle opener, or screwdriver, by all means pack them.

JUST IN CASE I'd recommend keeping sunscreen in your kit, even if you're not headed for especially sunny climes. The way the ozone layer works these days, even an afternoon's sightseeing cruise in Stockholm could result in a sunburned nose.

CHECK EXPIRATION DATES

The SPF protection in sunscreen loses its potency after a year; most products these days come imprinted with expiration dates. If you need fresh sunscreen for your trip, buy it before you go—the price is sure to be higher at that tourist-packed destination you're headed for.

BUG JUICE Some people recommend buying insect repellent in the country you are traveling to, rather than in the U.S., on the theory that each country knows best what works on its own native bugs. Not true, and possibly dangerous! The Food and Drug Administration was set up to protect U.S. citizens from the hazards of harmful medications, chemicals, and other substances; few other countries have an equivalent organization. Therefore, the repellent you buy overseas might contain ingredients outlawed for use in the United States—ingredients that may well be more harmful to you than to the mosquitoes themselves. Buy repellent in the United States, and plan to use it when needed, limiting your exposure to insects in other ways. Cover as much of your body as possible by wearing long-sleeved shirts (light-colored for coolness), long pants, and socks. Don't use perfumes or other scented products that may only make you more attractive to bugs. And stay inside during the hours when mosquitoes are hungriest, namely dawn and dusk.

WANT TO PACK A PUMP?

For toiletries stored in pump dispensers, tape a piece of cardboard between the pump and the lip of the bottle so that the pump cannot be depressed. (A dripping pump can be a real downer.)

STORING YOUR STASH Store your toiletries in a special case—one that's lined with plastic, please. Mine is soft-sided with two pockets; it's cherry red, and therefore impossible to miss among those white hotel towels (or beige, if the decorator felt absolutely daring). I load every toiletry item I need into this kit, so that I can simply bring the whole thing into the bathroom and leave it there—it saves me that desperate, dripping exit from the shower because my shampoo was still in the suitcase.

TO PACK OR NOT TO PACK: ELECTRICALS

Hair dryers are a major cause of night-before agonizing—do I pack it or not? If your hairstyle truly requires a blow-dry to look decent, call ahead to your hotel to see if dryers are provided—most upscale hotels these days have them. If you're a frequent traveler, it may be worth it for you to invest in a lightweight travel model, although even these can add significant bulk if you're going the total carry-on route. Hair dryers are heavy to tote along, and they require a converter abroad. I know more than one person who blew out the motor in a perfectly good hair dryer because she forgot to bring a current converter as well as a plug adapter.

What?

Yes, if you're going out of the country, you'll probably need both items—the converter to adapt the standard voltage at your destination into something your appliance can use, and the adapter to adapt the two-vertical-prong plug on the end of the electrical cord to fit local outlets.

Many foreign countries use a standard 220-volt current, which is different from the United States' 110 volts. The general rule of thumb is that the Eastern Hemisphere uses 220 volts, while Western Hemisphere countries use 110 volts, but there are plenty of exceptions—notably Argentina, Antigua, Chile, Guadaloupe, Honduras, Paraguay, St.Kitts/Nevis, St. Lucia, St. Vincent, and Uruguay, all of which use 220 volts even though they're in the Western Hemisphere.

As for plugs, there are five standard pin configurations:

- A, with flat parallel blades, like we use in the U.S.

- B, with two round pins, used in England and Germany.

- C, with three rectangular prongs, used in England and Hong Kong.

- D, with two round pins in a skinnier plug, à la France.

- E, with flat angled blades, found in Australia and New Zealand.

There is absolutely no rule of thumb to use here, except that A plugs are most common in the 110-volt countries. You'll be perfectly fine with your U.S. appliances in Canada, Mexico, Japan, Korea, Jamaica, Bermuda, and the Bahamas, as well as in U.S. territories such as Guam, Puerto Rico, and the U.S. Virgin Islands. Beyond that, it's a good idea to look up the electrical specifics of your destination in a travel guide before you go.

It's also essential to buy the adapters before you go—they won't be available in the country you're going to (there, stores sell adapters that change B pins to A pins, not the other way around).

Confused? Then take my basic advice: Think long and hard about whether you really need to take your appliances at all. If you need a computer for work, that's one thing, but if you can eliminate the hair dryer and shaver, you'll avoid the whole issue.

Some people enjoy getting perfume on their cotton balls, shoe polish on the swabs, and toothpaste all over everything. I don't. My foolproof tip for maintaining product individuality is . . . plastic sandwich bags, preferably the kind with the zipper tops. They're simply the perfect size for small products, and they stop leaks from spreading through the entire kit. If you really like to be organized, you can make "product pals" out of your toiletries—put your travel-size shampoo and conditioner into one sandwich bag, your disposable razor and travel-size shaving cream in another, etc. (This is even more fun at 3 AM when you have to leave for the airport at 5 AM and you haven't even begun ironing yet. Hey, would I lie? I've been there.)

After packing the kit with your sandwich-bagged toiletries, place it inside a large plastic bag as a final insurance against leakage, and then move on. If, after all this preparation, you still wind up with Brylcreem on your Bruno Maglis, something larger than both of us is at work.

SEAT MATE I prefer to take my toiletries kit on the plane, even when I have checked other luggage. The air in the cabin is pressurized and the kit is not manhandled by bagmen—two reasons why messy leaks and spills are less likely. Also, I like to have access to various items so that I can freshen up en route. Have you ever tried to convince a flight attendant to "dispense medication" (i.e., give you a Tylenol) for a headache? And if your luggage is delayed or lost, or gets whisked into storage at a hotel where your room isn't ready, it's nice to have a toothbrush handy, especially after an overseas flight.

▶ The Sewing Kit

It's a funny thing about sewing kits. I always thought they were, well, fussy, in a dowdy mother-hen kind of way. But there I was, in a panic because the hidden button had just fallen off my favorite wrap-around skirt—you know, the button that makes these garments look come-hither as opposed to come-and-get-it. So I telephoned the folks in

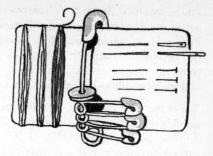

housekeeping, who happily reattached the button—for a price I prefer not to disclose. Moral of the story: Sewing kits do come in handy and they can save you lots and lots of money. They also don't take up much room.

WHAT'S IN YOUR SEWING KIT

- ❑ Thread—light, medium, and dark
- ❑ Buttons
- ❑ Safety pins—large and small
- ❑ Needles
- ❑ Small scissors

You can purchase a small sewing kit at your local five-and-dime or drugstore. Or make your own: String some small safety pins and a few buttons (small white and black ones are fine) onto a larger safety pin. Pierce a credit-card-size piece of cardboard with a needle and a few straight pins. Wind a supply of white, black, and navy thread around the cardboard, pin the button-bearing safety pin across the thread as if it were a belt, and you're in business. For scissors, you need look no farther than your Swiss Army knife—*see above*. (If you don't have one of these, nail scissors or small embroidery scissors will serve.) Place the card in a sandwich bag along with the scissors (or better yet, use one of those diminutive snack bags), then pack the whole thing into your toiletries kit. You'll always have it with you, and you'll be a hit with travelers who have forgotten theirs.

You of the male species, don't think you're exempt from needing this item. Sewing kits were standard issue for U.S. Army soldiers during World War II. If those guys could be expected to know how to sew, what's your excuse?

▶ The First-Aid Kit

I think my friend Pete possesses the nonpareil of first-aid kits. He keeps everything in an ancient metal Band-Aid box. Small yet serviceable, it has accompanied him everywhere from Belize to Bayonne, New Jersey. His kit includes gauze pads, adhesive strips, dental floss (also useful as spare

WHAT'S IN YOUR FIRST-AID KIT

- ❏ Acetaminophen
- ❏ Adhesive strips
- ❏ Antacid
- ❏ Anti-diarrheal pills
- ❏ Antiseptic towelettes
- ❏ Aspirin
- ❏ Birth control items
- ❏ Cold pills
- ❏ Gauze pads
- ❏ Medications you need
- ❏ Moleskin

shoelaces or thread), pre-moistened antiseptic towelettes (for sterilizing and cleaning cuts and abrasions), even a spare roll of film. There's enough of each of the medications in Pete's kit—cold pills, anti-diarrheal pills, antacid, aspirin, acetaminophen—to last two days, as he figures that

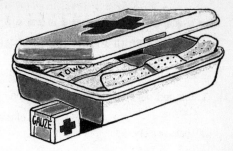

if you do fall ill on the road, you should be able to locate more specific medical treatment in that time. You will probably need additional items if you plan to hike, camp, or otherwise travel in the forest, jungle, or other terrain away from civilization.

It's also a good idea to make sure you've got adequate birth control with you. Often, the moment you need it is long after the shops have closed, and even then, it's not always available.

▶ The Personal Documents Kit

Maintain a pouch or envelope for miscellaneous travel documents, including any leftover traveler's checks, copies of prescriptions for medications and eyeglasses, a list of your credit card numbers, and important phone numbers (family, neighbors, doctors, work associates). Add to this a photocopy of the first page of your passport. If you don't have such documents on hand, get out your address book, stop by a photocopier, and put it all together now, whether or not you've got a trip in the offing. Even if you never get robbed or fall ill in a foreign country, being prepared is worth it for the peace of mind alone. Keep the envelope in your luggage. Give a copy of the first page of your passport to a friend at home.

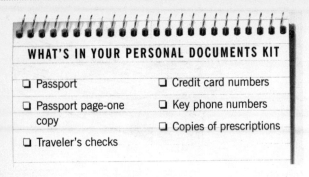

WHAT'S IN YOUR PERSONAL DOCUMENTS KIT

- ❏ Passport
- ❏ Passport page-one copy
- ❏ Traveler's checks
- ❏ Credit card numbers
- ❏ Key phone numbers
- ❏ Copies of prescriptions

When it's time to travel, just add your airline tickets, hotel reservations documents or any other confirmations of prepaid travel information, maps of your destination, your guidebook, and more traveler's checks and you're on your way.

❭ The Portable Office

Having a small kit of often-used business items can save time and be a real convenience on the road.

Bring letter-size envelopes to hold receipts as well as for correspondence, and 10" by 13" manila envelopes, come in handy for sending brochures and papers home, so that you don't have to pack them in your luggage. Use one of these envelopes as a pouch for all of the other material on this list. Keep all the small items in a resealable plastic bag.

You need only replenish items as needed. Then the next time a business associate cries, "A paper clip! A paper clip! My MBA for a paper clip!" you can reach into your kit and smugly save the day.

WHAT'S IN YOUR PORTABLE OFFICE

- ❏ Business cards
- ❏ Calculator
- ❏ Clear tape
- ❏ Duct tape
- ❏ Envelopes
- ❏ Eraser
- ❏ A notepad
- ❏ Paper clips
- ❏ Pens and pencils
- ❏ Small pencil sharpener
- ❏ Postage stamps
- ❏ Resealable plastic bags
- ❏ Rubber bands
- ❏ Self-adhesive notes
- ❏ Miniature stapler
- ❏ Stationery
- ❏ Tape
- ❏ Telephone calling card
- ❏ Telephone access code list

▶ For Passionate Shoppers

It may be a replica birchbark canoe, spied at an outfitters' store at the end of a week in Canada's Quetico wilderness. Or it may be three matching china vegetable dishes, complete with lids, which you find for a song at a Paris flea market. Or some other must-have. But you'd better face it from the get-go: Even if you hate to shop, you'll probably find something you can't live without, some time in

SHOPPERS' SURVIVAL KIT

- ❏ Bubble wrap
- ❏ Scissors
- ❏ Tape
- ❏ Tote bag

your vacation. If you intend to do some serious shopping, don't leave home without bubble wrap, scissors, tape, and a totally collapsible tote bag. The former is useful for anything that's even vaguely breakable—even when it might well be easy to find, who wants to waste valuable vacation time looking for a Staples? The latter will make it easy to consolidate your purchases and get them onto the plane.

▶ The Toy Tote

Traveling with young children? Then plan to bring a carry-on full of toys, books, and activities. Even if you're taking a car trip, a portable toy stash for the back seat can be a godsend. Holly, a travel writer who has three young children, keeps on hand a large tote devoted to travel toys—one-piece items that a sitting child can fiddle with happily for several minutes at a time. ("One-piece" is the operative term—ever try to pick up fifty tiny Lego bricks from underneath an airplane seat?) Her tote includes everything from hand-held electronic games and Silly Putty to those cheap little puzzles with sliding tiles in a plastic tray, a Magic Slate (lift the gray film layer and your picture goes bye-bye), and a Woolly Willy (use a magnet to put metal-shaving hair and whiskers on bald Willy).

Karen swears by coloring/activity books and a small clipboard with note pad and pencils (good for tic-tac-toe, hangman, math practice, etc.). She packs one of these kits for each of her two daughters in a gallon-size resealable plastic bag. She takes crayons and washable markers on airplanes, colored pencils on car trips. "Never let your kids have crayons in the car in summer," she warns, "unless you don't mind having melted wax in odd cracks and crevices." And watch out for nonwashable markers anywhere. The odd uncapped marker is sure to slip unnoticed out of your child's hand, only to bleed profusely on your car's beige upholstery or—worse—on your husband's expensive light wool trousers.

Both moms are always on the lookout for new items to add to their totes, and they never let their kids get into the bags between trips, lest they wear out their interest in those particular toys. Holly recounts a plane trip to Florida when her family sat behind a couple with a two-year-old boy who screamed and wailed for the first half hour of the flight. Finally, Holly reached over the seat and started handing him toys from her tote. The parents were astonished to find that their child remained quiet so long as he was entertained.

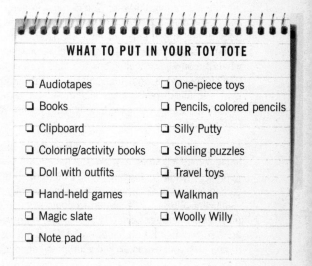

WHAT TO PUT IN YOUR TOY TOTE

- ❏ Audiotapes
- ❏ Books
- ❏ Clipboard
- ❏ Coloring/activity books
- ❏ Doll with outfits
- ❏ Hand-held games
- ❏ Magic slate
- ❏ Note pad
- ❏ One-piece toys
- ❏ Pencils, colored pencils
- ❏ Silly Putty
- ❏ Sliding puzzles
- ❏ Travel toys
- ❏ Walkman
- ❏ Woolly Willy

A TASTE OF HOME

Some travelers like to pack a few food items they know are hard to find when they're away from home. I'm talking easy-to-pack stuff—unlike Kathy, a woman I know who routinely loads her suitcase with cans of tuna and jars of peanut butter when she takes long business trips to Asia (she's the only person I know who hates Chinese food). Herbal tea bags, on the other hand, are small and light, and can really provide a soothing lift when you're most in need of one. If you can't tolerate caffeine, it might be wise to pack some single-cup portions of instant decaffeinated coffee to get you through those occasions when the only java available is the kind with a jolt. Remember your favorite sugar substitute, too—Equal comes in pill dispensers the size of Tic Tac boxes. These little things can go a long way to making you feel more at home on the road.

Acting on the same principle, I always try to bring along something small to make the hotel room seem homier. A family picture (it needn't be framed) or a stuffed animal to sleep with at night instead of your significant other—these can do wonders to brighten up a sterile setting. Scented candles and bath salts are also nice to have on hand. And if this is a honeymoon, may your extras exceed your imagination!

Countdown to Packing

Isn't it exciting? You're almost on vacation...and you've taken care of everything I've suggested so far, right? I certainly hope so, because we're about to add to the list.

YOUR PRE-TRIP TO-DO LIST

- ❏ Do laundry
- ❏ Pick up dry cleaning
- ❏ Collect packing aids
- ❏ Get out your luggage
- ❏ Convert $50–$100 to foreign currency
- ❏ Buy traveler's checks
- ❏ Set aside $1 bills for tips
- ❏ Update your travel documents kit
- ❏ Replenish toiletry kit
- ❏ Replace expired medications/sunscreen

The first thing to do is to start to collect packing helpers such as tissue paper, plastic dry-cleaning bags, and resealable plastic bags—sandwich- and gallon-size. The latter will isolate wet bathing suits or other objects, or hold together collections of small objects you may gather in your travels—seashells, business cards, etc.

Open your luggage and place it on the floor in your bedroom, so you can pre-pack items as you remember them. If you are using a new garment bag, experiment to discover which hangers work best with it. If you don't have the right ones, get them now.

Convert enough foreign currency to allow you to hail a cab from the airport to your hotel ($50 to $100 should do it—ask for small bills). Arrange to put most of your money into traveler's checks. Traveling twosomes (friends, spouses, family members) may want to check out American Express Traveler's Checks for Two—either party can sign a check without requiring the other to witness, so you can each go your own way occasionally.

Begin setting aside $1 bills to use as tips while on the road—it saves having to struggle with minute amounts of an unfamiliar currency. Throughout the Caribbean and in many cruise ports, dollars are happily accepted. If you're traveling to Europe or Asia, however, it's better to deal in deutschmarks, francs, or yen from the get-go.

Designate a specific place for your travel documents: passport, airline tickets, traveler's checks. Add items as you remember them.

Tuck the empty resealable bags into your suitcase, along with a large plastic or mesh bag to keep dirty clothes separate from clean ones along the way. Also, pack a lightweight tote bag to use as a day pack or to carry new purchases in on the trip back home.

Check on the status of your travel kits (*see above*). Replenish toiletry items as needed, replace expired medications (remember to check the expiration date on your sunscreen, too!), and add new items specific to the upcoming trip.

PACKING FOR A FAMILY

Depending on their ages, you may wish to include your children in the packing process by encouraging them to bring you what they consider to be appropriate clothing and toys. (Happy camper tip: Try not to laugh in front of the kids.) Or you may wish to spend some quality time with each of them and supervise their choices, remembering that asking your children to help can backfire. "If I let them choose," says my cousin Donna of her children, "they forget something important, like socks. Sometimes, it's a guessing game: If I don't pack what I know they'll want even though they've forgotten it, they'll wind up blaming mommy. So if everyone is to be happy—including me—I find it's easier simply to pack for them." Michael, father of two, agrees. "If my children choose a relatively new toy, I always pack a tried-and-true one as well," he says. "Nine times out of ten, they want the comfort of the old one, and are they glad to find it waiting for them!"

The packing situation gets exponentially pricklier with teenagers. Theoretically, a teenager ought to be able to handle this job, and if you've got kids this age you know how they resent parental involvement. Still, their judgment may not always be totally reliable. ("Mom, I'll die rather than wear that flowered dress. You know I like my overalls better, and I'm sure no one at the wedding will care.") A good middle road may be to review their packing list ahead of time, making tactful suggestions. (Better still, inspect the suitcase once it's packed when your teen isn't around to protest).

▶ The Night Before

We're not saying you should plan to pull an all-night packing session. But clothing does wrinkle and needs to breathe, so it's best to pack as close to your departure time as possible—your clothes will thank you.

YOUR NIGHT-BEFORE TO-DO LIST

❑ Put on mood music

❑ Set up your ironing board

❑ Lay out your clothing

❑ Weed out the excess

❑ Iron everything you're taking

❑ Fasten all the fastenings

❑ Pack everything

❑ Put your final packing list in your carry-on

Since packing can be stressful, think about creating the packing environment that's just right for you. You may wish to light some scented candles and listen to Kenny G. Or you may prefer to crank up the Rolling Stones and knock back a long-neck bottle of beer. You may desire silence. You'll definitely need an ironing board.

Set up your ironing board near a large, flat space such as a table top or bed. (In my case, of course, my ironing board *is* my bed. But that's another story.) Lay out all of the clothing you plan to take and look it over. Most packers claim that this is the critical moment, when you should remove half of the clothing and pack only the remaining half. I suggest you do this a little less painfully: Just keep refining your list, weeding out extras and single-use items. As you work with your assembled wardrobe, a certain logic—call it the Zen of Packing—will come to your aid and allow you to make the correct choices.

One more pointer. When you've finished pruning down your list, cross off your last-minute deletions and slip a copy of the list in your briefcase, purse, or carry-on. It will prove invaluable to you if your luggage is lost or stolen.

KEEP OLD LISTS

Once you've returned from your trip, keep your list in a pocket of your luggage so you can consult it the next time you travel. You may need to add or delete items to suit the itinerary, but the basic list may well remain the same.

Iron all your clothing. If you start out with a well-pressed piece, the chances of its creasing en route are, well, decreased—no matter what the luggage or how long the trip. Ironed clothes also lie flatter and thus take up less space. Place ironed clothing on hangers until you are ready to fold.

Finally, button up. Fasten every button, zip every zipper, and hook every hook of your clothing. It makes all the difference for a shirt placket to lie for eight hours as God and Ralph Lauren intended, as opposed to being bent or folded unnaturally.

And now you're ready to pack.

Get Packing!

I know two women—college roommates and fast friends—who agree on almost everything except how to pack a suitcase. One is convinced that she can get more stuff in by spreading her clothes absolutely flat in the bottom of the case; the other is a passionate devotee of the rolling-up school of thought. In college, they argued about this every time they packed their bags—every Christmas, every spring break, every June. And you know what? Twenty years later, they still argue about it every time they take their families to visit each other.

▶ How to Fill Almost Any Suitcase

The truth is, each type of garment can be folded in a different way, and each bag lends itself to a different method of packing. So who says you can't teach an old dog new tricks? In the following pages, you'll learn to do the "dressmaker's dummy," the "roll," and the "interlock," among other systems of packing that ensure a well-packed piece of luggage, whether it hangs, rolls, or rides on your back.

ROCK AND ROLL Rolling is an easy way to pack clothing, both light and heavy. It works best for duffels and travel packs, but if your trip is casual, you can roll garments for standard suitcases as well.

Let's demonstrate with a T-shirt: Lay the shirt facedown on a flat surface. Fold in the sleeves. Then, with the shirt still facedown, begin to roll it up from the bottom hem. Smooth it as you go, so that no wrinkles are folded in. The collar should wind up on the outside of the roll.

Jeans are a natural for this process. Even dress slacks can be rolled: Hold them upside down, by the cuffs, and lay them out, then roll from the cuffs up. Bruce, who almost always packs in a travel pack, even rolls sports jackets: Fold the jacket in half lengthwise, tucking the arms inside, then begin at the top and roll down.

Delicate garments should be placed on top of T-shirts or tissue paper before being rolled. I myself have had great luck rolling a piqué sundress by filling the dress with a plastic dry-cleaning bag, backing and fronting it with two more bags, then rolling it from the hem up. Skirts can be done this way as well: Put a plastic dry-cleaning bag inside the skirt to pad it, then either roll it, or fold it in half lengthwise over another garment to pad the crease, then roll. Soon, you'll be able to roll anything.

THE INTERLOCK The theory behind the interlock, which works best with standard suitcases and travel packs, is that each piece of clothing folds over or is cushioned by another piece. My cousin Valerie explained this to me as I watched her pack for her return to college during the winter of 1981. It's really quite simple: Lay a pair of slacks or a skirt across an open suitcase from north to south, allowing some surplus to drape over each side. Place a sweater from east to west, allowing arms to drape both east and west and tail to drape to the south. Now flip the northern part of the slacks over the top of the sweater, fold the sweater arms in over this, then fold the bottom of the sweater and the southern part of the slacks or skirt over everything. You've created a neat stack of clothing that provides cushioning everywhere a wrinkle wants to be. You can add as few or as many garments to this construction as you wish. When you're done, fill in the corners and crevices with underwear, socks, scarves, etc. Place shoes (stuffed, please) heel down along the hinges of your suitcase.

PORTABLE SCRAPBOOK

Florida's Patricia Fairchild won an award in Wyndham Hotels' search for the savviest women business travelers for her tip: She always packs a photo of her suitcase in her briefcase, just in case the airline loses it.

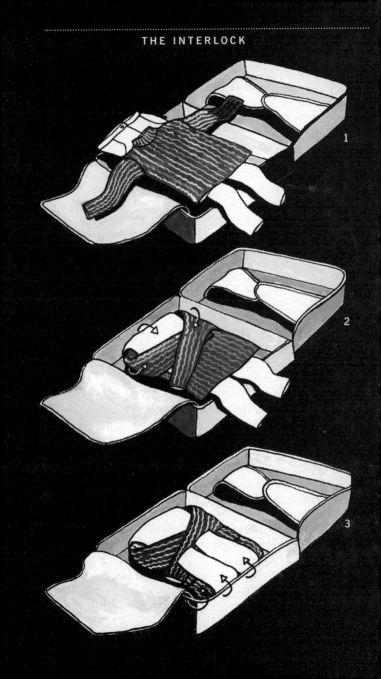

USE YOUR SHOES!

Shoes should never be empty—they should always be stuffed with underwear, socks, a child's shoe, a purse-size travel umbrella. . . . Otherwise, the hollows of your shoes are just wasted space, and those small items are free to wriggle into whatever crevice they please. We all harbor fears that a customs official will fling open our suitcase, revealing our Victoria's Secret teddy or heart-dappled boxer shorts to the airport community at large; stuff them in a shoe and he'll never notice. Depending on how fancy you want to get, you can buy cloth drawstring shoe bags, or you can simply place each shoe in its own plastic shopping bag. But do pack shoes separately rather than as a pair—they offer greater positioning possibilities that way.

TWIN TOWERS, AND A CHRONOLOGICAL APPROACH This is the way that most people put clothing into their luggage. Fold your clothes, using the folding techniques described below, then place them in the case in two neat stacks. If you know your trip schedule, pile them chronologically—the first day's outfit on top, the second day's clothes below that, and so forth. This will eliminate the need to paw through everything to unearth that purple polo shirt you meant to wear in the opening-day golf tournament. Fill in around the edges and in the center with underwear and socks, bathing suits, etc. Try to pack snugly so that things will not move around in the suitcase. If your suitcase has interior straps that you can use to secure clothing, use them.

Alternatively, you can roll your clothes and then stack them neatly like cigarettes in a box. Again, if you lay them in so that the things you plan to wear first are on top, you'll have the easiest time getting to your gear.

When you pack clothing into a pullman, you can fold and stack, roll and stack, or use a combination of these methods.

LET'S HEAR IT FOR PLASTIC!

TIP

One of life's little injustices is that whether you fill a suitcase by upending the contents of your dresser drawer into the main compartment, or by folding and neatly laying things in, you will have wrinkles. And whether they are the chaotic wrinkles that mark a dumper or the organized wrinkles of someone who has packed carefully, you'll lack that bandbox-fresh look that you'd have at home. (In fact, you can end up with wrinkles even if a garment bag is your luggage of choice.) Although some packing experts swear that tissue paper yields the most crease-free packing, I never contemplate leaving home without plastic. It works every time.

So when trip time approaches, start saving plastic dry cleaner bags. And use them for everything that you want to roll, fold, or hang wrinkle-free.

Using a garment bag? Start with a hanger with an empty dry cleaner bag over it. Add a dress. Then top it with a second dry cleaner bag. If you want, you can make this ensemble the base of a dressmaker's dummy (see below). Each time you add a new garment, either add another plastic bag or use each garment to pad the next—pull shirt sleeves through vest armholes, for example.

Packing in a duffel or pullman? Put a plastic bag inside and outside wrinkle-prone clothing to provide extra padding. I have a colleague who does the dressmaker's dummy with plastic for her business clothing—and then rolls the package into a bundle and throws it into a beat-up duffel.

Plastic is the answer. Trust me on this.

◗ For Duffels and Travel Packs

The challenge with duffels and travel packs is twofold: the soft-sided construction and the large single compartment. There is little to keep clothing from being squashed, and items can become disorganized and sometimes even "lost" in the bottom. Often you have to unpack and repack to get at small items. There are two ways to prevent this. One is to perfect the "roll" for clothing (*see above*). The other is to investigate travel organizers that effectively partition the space so that items remain in place and are protected.

THE KEY—DISTRIBUTE THE WEIGHT After rolling all your clothing, give some thought to how you plan to carry your luggage. With a duffel, since you usually use a shoulder strap or top handles, pack your heaviest items, such as shoes, on the bottom. Then put in your rolls of clothing, either horizontally or vertically.

To fill travel packs, most people lay them down like a standard suitcase. But then, when on one's back, where they are usually carried, everything tends to slip out of place. Remember this simple fact when you pack, and start the process by standing your pack up in a chair so that it looks more like a shelf.

THE ZONE SYSTEM As I mentioned above, the large central space of a duffel or pack can be a real problem when it comes to smaller items. My friend Bennett once spent 20 minutes searching around his hotel room for his black socks—which were in the bottom of his black duffel. Steve, a veteran duffel man, has another solution. The zone system, as he calls it, consists of mesh bags of all sizes—Steve buys those mesh laundry bags made for sweaters, lingerie, and other delicate items, which he finds in stores like Woolworth, Kmart, and Caldor. The mesh bags dry quickly when wet, allow air to get at the clothes when it's hot, and are see-through enough so you can find what you're looking for pretty quickly. Steve uses a different bag for each clothing type;

all the socks go into one bag, all the shirts go into another, etc. Once he's finished sorting, he throws all the bags into his duffel and gets going. When he needs something, he finds it quickly, and barely disturbs anything else. During the trip, he can re-sort what's in the bags to keep dirty laundry separate from clean stuff.

A famous pack maker has another answer to the open space problem: an accessory that resembles a center rectangle with four flaps attached to it. You stack all your carefully folded clothing onto the center rectangle, add a companion rectangle on top, then flip each of the four flaps over both boards and snap them all into place, in effect making a sandwich of your clothing. It helps keep important clothing from sliding around in the large compartment of a duffel or travel pack.

ONE MORE HANDY TIP Stick your reading material in the pack's outside pockets—not only so that you can easily reach it en route, but also so that it will provide a hard shell to protect your clothing.

▶ Know-How for Garment Baggers

The advantage of a garment bag is that your clothes can be kept neatly on hangers, ready to transfer to a hotel closet. But because these bags are soft-sided and don't have much of a frame, clothes are easily crushed and creased in them. Shrewd packing can reduce this problem.

YOUR BASIC HANG-UPS Items fresh from the dry cleaner can go straight into the garment bag. When hanging a single garment on a hanger, first place a dry-cleaning bag over the hanger—this will protect the garment from resting directly on the hanger as well as providing a little stuffing, or cushioning, to help keep the garment's shape. Add garment, stuff sleeves with tissue paper if needed, then encase in plastic. (Note: The plastic bag traps air, which will help to cushion this garment from the one you'll place on top of it. While you may pack a garment bag vertically, it does not remain that way; once the bag is

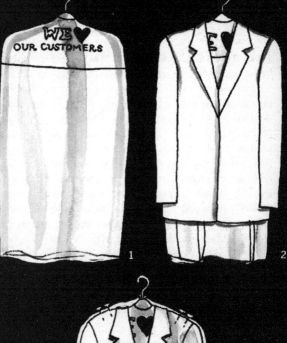

closed, folded, and stowed, items lie directly on top of one another.) Does one stubborn garment keep slipping off the hanger? Try securing it with clothespins or straight pins, taking care to pin on an unseen part of the garment, to prevent crimping.

THE DRESSMAKER'S DUMMY Veteran packers know this technique can maximize the clothing you pack with a minimum of hangers, while cutting down on creases. Begin with a bare hanger. Put a T-shirt over it. Add a dress. Pull the arms of the T-shirt through the arms of the dress. Cover with a vest, sweater, or jacket. (Try to plan it so that these various pieces actually make up one real outfit—this way, you can save time when unpacking and can just grab a single hanger.) Encase in a dry-cleaning bag. If you are packing pants, use a hanger with a padded bar, or pad the bar of the hanger with a T-shirt or sweater, so that you don't put too sharp a crease in your trousers when you drape them over the bar. (Tie technique #1: Add a matching tie now, draping it over your slacks.) Cover with a long-sleeved shirt, then add a jacket. Pull the sleeves of the shirt through the jacket sleeves. (Tie technique #2: Roll up a matching tie, then slip it into your jacket pocket.) You can also do the dressmaker's dummy outfit by outfit; group coordinating accessories for each one in a resealable plastic bag; then poke a hole in the bag to slip it over the top of the hanger. Encase all in plastic, and proceed to next outfit.

1

2

3

HOW TO PACK TIES

Some men prefer to roll them up and put them in shoes. Others buy nifty tie holder cases. (C'mon guys, these add weight!) My friend Bruce, the sports-jacket roller—who'd be pretty put out if his ties were creased—swears by rolling them and slipping them into a jacket pocket, or laying them flat inside the sleeve of a jacket. If you're packing in a garment bag, you can simply drape your ties over a padded hanger bar.

KEEP IT CREASE-FREE I like to hang the longest garments in the bag first, then follow with the shorter ones. This way, when the tails of the longer garments are folded to fit into the bag, they are cushioned by the hems of the shorter garments. To prevent a crease, you can also pad the fold with wrinkle-free items such as underwear, socks, or bathing suits. Hang delicate items in the middle of the bag, not in the front or back, so that they are not wrinkled when the bag is closed and folded in half. Before closing the bag, lay two more dry-cleaning bags over the clothing to protect against crimping from the internal straps.

KEY TRAVEL ACCESSORIES Look for a hanging organizer with a fabric back and see-through plastic pockets, similar to an oversize jewelry roll. This is ideal for pantyhose, scarves, slips, and other items. The hook on top allows you to hang it in the garment bag as well as in your hotel closet. The see-through plastic saves you time spent searching for things.

Most heavy-duty garment bags have inside compartments for shoes (stuffed, please) and other gear.

WHAT NOT TO PACK I strongly advise against packing toiletries in a garment bag you plan to check. There is simply too much risk of the bag being mishandled, causing all kinds of leaks and spillage. Bring toiletries on board the airplane. If you must pack them in your checked garment bag, I suggest lining the compartment with a plastic bag. Then, light a candle to the patron saint of lost causes—you are simply asking for trouble!

And don't place anything of value in the outside pockets of your garment bag, unless they lock. This is a good place for books, shoes, socks, and other mundane items that would give a thief an instant case of ennui.

A BONUS FOR GARMENT BAGGERS If you are checking your garment bag, some airlines provide a free rectangular cardboard box that allows your garment bag to lie flat instead of being folded in half. The cardboard provides a hard shell for the soft-sided bag and protects it from the horrors of the cargo hold.

▶ Practically Crease-Free Folding

No matter what kind of luggage you use, the time eventually comes when you'll need to fold something—perhaps even the dreaded long-sleeved Oxford-cloth shirt. Using a few tried-and-true methods, you can keep wrinkling to a minimum.

TOPS: THE CLOTHING-STORE METHOD At a well-known nationwide casual clothing chain that shall remain nameless (aw, you guessed it!), long-sleeve button-down shirts are folded in the following way: Button all the buttons, including the top-collar button. Place the shirt facedown on a flat surface. Bring in the left side of the shirt body about 2 or 3 inches and fold. Take the arm and fold it straight down, parallel to the shirt body, with the cuff at the shirttail; line up the outer edge of the arm with the edge of the shirt body. Do the same for the right side. Bring the shirttail section up a third of the way, then fold over again, so that when you turn the shirt over, the collar is on top.

TOPS: THE DRY-CLEANER METHOD Yes, your fearless author actually watched, fascinated, as a neighborhood dry-cleaning wizard worked his magic folding

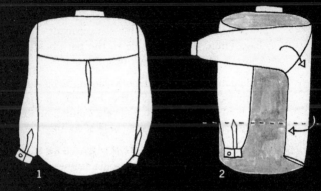

1 2

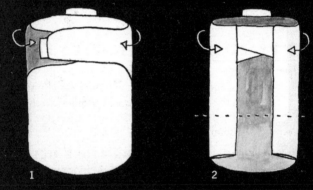

1 2

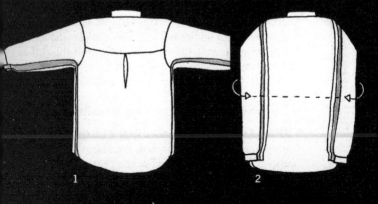

1 2

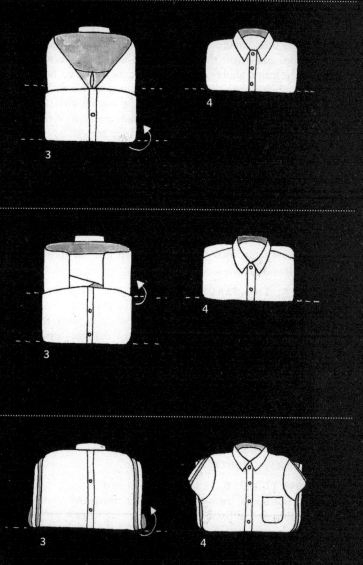

machine. And unlike most television stunts, you actually can try this at home. Begin as directed above: Button the buttons and lay the shirt facedown. Then, without bending the shirt body, bring the left arm of the shirt to lie horizontally across the top back of the shirt, so that you're creasing it at the shoulder joint. Do the same with the right sleeve. (If sleeves are longer than the body of the shirt is wide, try folding each sleeve in at the cuff.) Fold the left side of the shirt in about 2 or 3 inches, then fold the right side. Bring shirttail section up a third of the way, then fold over again, so that when you turn the shirt over, the collar is on top. While this method requires a few extra folds, and folds have a way of becoming creases, many men insist that this is their favorite method. My suspicion is that they don't actually fold the shirts themselves; it's just easier to pack a shirt when it's fresh from the dry cleaner.

TOPS: THE STACK-AND-FOLD METHOD Stack several buttoned shirts atop one another, facedown on a flat surface, and proceed to fold them all as one: Bend the left arm at the shoulder joint and bring it down to lie parallel with the shirt body, cuff touching shirttail. Do the same with the right arm. Then bring the shirttail up to meet the collar.

ESPECIALLY FOR LONG-SLEEVE SWEATERS Put your sweater facedown on a flat surface. Bending the sweater only at the shoulder joint, fold the arms in to lie horizontally across top back of sweater. Then bring the bottom up to meet the top.

HOW TO FOLD SLACKS Lay slacks on a flat surface and line up the legs so that the center creases meet, both in front and in back. Bring the outer leg halfway up so that the corner of the outer cuff touches the back pocket, and bring the inner leg up to align with the front pocket (this eliminates some bulk). You can then fold the slacks in half again.

HOW TO PACK A SUN HAT

TIP.

Some people prefer to bring their sun hats with them, while others prefer to buy a hat once they're in a foreign country—it's a nice way to support the local economy, and is a lasting souvenir of the trip. Either way, however, you'll need to pack it. Here goes: The sun hat should be filled with clothing—underwear and socks are great for this, and they are then hidden from the eyes of the customs man—and the hat placed in the suitcase as if you were wearing it. Now, take some rolled clothing and tuck it around the brim, or fill in to keep the shape of a wire-brim. Pack the rest of your clothing around and over the hat. It will have been padded enough to retain its shape.

▶ Packing Carry-Ons

Although guidelines vary from airline to airline, most allow you to carry on two bags, each one able to fit either in an overhead compartment or below the seat in front of you. Computers and camera/video bags are generally included in this count, along with carry-on suitcases or garment bags; pocketbooks, coats, diaper bags, and umbrellas are generally not. Larger items, including garment bags, infant car seats, and strollers, may have to be stowed in the small closet at the front of the cabin—and believe me, this space fills up fast, so don't depend on being allowed to use it. If your carry-on doesn't fit in the cabin, you'll have to check it. Be sure to ask the flight attendant whether the airline will whiz it straight down to the cargo hold (standard in most cases) or hold it and send it on another flight.

IF YOUR ONLY LUGGAGE IS A CARRY-ON If you plan to pack everything you need for your trip into a cabin carry-on, efficient packing techniques are really important: check out the roll method and the interlock; if you're taking a duffel or travel pack, use chronological stacking or the zone method (*see* For Duffels and Travel Packs, *above*) to make it easy to locate what you need when you need it.

If your under-the-seat carry-on is soft-sided, it's a good idea to lay any books or magazines you've brought for in-flight reading on top—they're easier to reach that way, and they'll create an extra layer of protection for your gear when you shove your bag under the seat in front of you.

Plan to reserve heavy articles for your under-the-seat bag rather than the one you'll be stowing overhead. Com-partment doors do occasionally pop open mid-flight, and weighty items increase the chance of your bag's toppling out (possibly onto your own head—ouch!). Even if that doesn't happen, you don't want to hoist a heavy load over your head to get it into (and out of) the compartment in the first place.

ONCE IN YOUR HOTEL ROOM

Try to unpack as completely as possible as soon as possible so your clothing has a chance to breathe and wrinkles can fall out naturally. On a trip in which I changed hotels every night for six nights, I packed in a garment bag. The minute I got to the room I would remove only what I needed for the evening and the following morning. Even this small amount of breath-ing room cut down on last-minute pressing.

Finally, always prepare at least one of your carry-on pieces as though you might have to check it—label it, lock it, and remove anything that doesn't belong in checked lug-gage. Then, when you end up bringing home an extra shopping tote packed with a plaster-of-Paris replica of the Parthenon (complete with three-dimensional centaurs in the pediments), you can check your original carry-on bag with some peace of mind.

WHAT TO CARRY ON WHEN YOU CHECK LUGGAGE

❏ Bathing suit

❏ Breakables

❏ Camera, exposed film

❏ Change of clothing

❏ Gifts

❏ Guidebook

❏ In-flight reading

❏ In-flight travel accessories

❏ Laptop, fully charged

❏ Personal documents kit

❏ Toiletries kit

❏ Valuables

❏ Walkman, audiotapes

❏ Work materials

WHAT TO CARRY WHEN YOU CHECK LUGGAGE
Even if you're checking other bags, you'll probably also be taking a carry-on into the passenger cabin with you. Among other things, it should always include anything too valuable to consign to the cargo hold—such as jewelry, prescription medications, and your spare pair of eyeglasses—and anything too breakable to consign to the cargo hold. (Regarding these last two points, it's a good bet that some of the souvenirs or gifts you'll buy during your trip will fall into these categories. Plan to have more

A WORD ABOUT COURTESY

The carry-on concept may have begun after Amy Vanderbilt and Emily Post had their say, but as more travelers opt to carry their luggage aboard and as airlines continue to cut back on the size of overhead compartments and under-seat legroom, your fellow passengers will thank you for observing a few heretofore unwritten rules of carry-on etiquette.

Most important, remember that one overhead compartment serves two and sometimes three passengers. Your baggage should not fill the entire compartment; try to leave room for someone else's stuff as well.

If you are asked to check your luggage after boarding, try to cooperate with the flight attendant. Most likely, he or she has asked you to do so because your luggage really is too large, or perhaps because the flight is full. Anticipate this situation by locking your luggage.

room in your carry-on for the return trip than you did coming out.)

You'll also want to have in-flight reading material as well as any in-flight travel accessories you want to use—an inflatable neck pillow, a sleeping mask, slippers, etc.

Less obviously, it's a good idea to put in any gifts you've brought for whoever's meeting you at your destination, and a change of clothing, just in case your luggage gets lost—or something gets spilled all over you during the flight. (Turbulence happens, and so do clumsy flight attendants.)

And if your destination is the Caribbean or some other sunspot, why not add your bathing suit—it's light and takes up very little space. If, say, you've landed in Jamaica but your checked luggage hasn't, what do you care if you've got your bathing suit? Go and bask on a luscious bit of beach while your bags are being located.

3

THE PACKING
LIST

The wish list, the wait list, the black list, the "A"
list...sometimes it seems our lives are governed by
lists. But they really do come in handy when
packing, especially when you're preparing for a
last-minute trip. Remember that lists can be used
twice—once to pack and once to repack—so
you'll be sure to remember to take home everything you've brought with you (*see* Chapter 4).

Your Wardrobe

Although everyone has his or her own clothing style and packing priorities, there is a core group of items every traveler needs. The basic lists in this chapter should help you focus your thinking. Under headings thereafter are a series of tips to further define your choices. Of course these are simply guidelines. Edit this list according to the length of your stay, climate of your destination, the season, and the purpose of your trip. (And remember that at least one outfit won't go in your suitcase but will be worn in transit.)

Women should remember the virtues of mixing and matching. Choose one color scheme, and opt for separates over one-piece dresses; accentuate with accessories. Reusing a few items in a variety of combinations can help you adapt.

A CRASH COURSE IN PACKING

- ❏ Find out what your hotel provides.
- ❏ Follow weather reports for your destination.
- ❏ Organize your wardrobe around a color scheme.
- ❏ Match clothing to your itinerary and destination.
- ❏ Keep several travel kits.
- ❏ Lay out each outfit before packing.
- ❏ Learn to fold.

BASIC WARDROBE FOR MEN

SUITS, JACKETS
- ❑ Blazer
- ❑ Sport coat
- ❑ Suits

TROUSERS
- ❑ Casual slacks
- ❑ Dress pants
- ❑ Jeans
- ❑ Shorts

SHIRTS
- ❑ Casual shirts
- ❑ Dress shirts
- ❑ Polo shirts
- ❑ T-shirts
- ❑ Turtlenecks

SWEATERS
- ❑ Cardigans
- ❑ Pullovers
- ❑ Sweater vest

ACCESSORIES
- ❑ Belts
- ❑ Cufflinks
- ❑ Pocket squares
- ❑ Sunglasses
- ❑ Suspenders
- ❑ Ties

SHOES
- ❑ Boots
- ❑ Dress shoes
- ❑ Sandals
- ❑ Sneakers, athletic shoes
- ❑ Walking shoes
- ❑ Water shoes, thongs

SOCKS
- ❑ Athletic socks
- ❑ Dress socks

UNDERWEAR
- ❑ Boxers, briefs
- ❑ Long johns
- ❑ T-shirts

SLEEPWEAR
- ❑ Pajamas
- ❑ Robe
- ❑ Slippers

FOR SPORTS

❑ Bathing suits

❑ Sports equipment

❑ Swim goggles

❑ T-shirt or cover-up

❑ Workout gear

FOR EVENING

❑ Cufflinks

❑ Cummerbund

❑ Dressy shoes

❑ Studs

❑ Tie

❑ Tux

❑ Tux shirt

❑ Vest

OUTERWEAR

❑ Baseball cap

❑ Gloves

❑ Overcoat

❑ Parka

❑ Raincoat, zip-out lining

❑ Scarf

❑ Sun hat

❑ Tote bag

❑ Umbrella

❑ Windbreaker

❑ Winter hat

BASIC WARDROBE FOR WOMEN

BUSINESS WEAR

- ❑ Dresses
- ❑ Suits

JACKETS

- ❑ Blazer
- ❑ Other jackets

TROUSERS

- ❑ Casual slacks
- ❑ Dress pants
- ❑ Jeans
- ❑ Shorts

SKIRTS

- ❑ Casual skirts
- ❑ Dress skirts

SHIRTS

- ❑ Blouses
- ❑ Casual shirts
- ❑ Knit tops
- ❑ Polo shirts
- ❑ T-shirts
- ❑ Turtlenecks

DRESSES

- ❑ Casual dresses
- ❑ Sundresses

SWEATERS

- ❑ Cardigans
- ❑ Pullovers
- ❑ Sweater vest

ACCESSORIES

- ❑ Belts
- ❑ Cufflinks
- ❑ Earrings, necklaces
- ❑ Hair ties, barrettes
- ❑ Scarves
- ❑ Sunglasses

SHOES

- ❑ Boots
- ❑ Dress heels
- ❑ Flats
- ❑ Walking shoes
- ❑ Sandals
- ❑ Sneakers, athletic shoes
- ❑ Water shoes, thongs

SOCKS

- ❑ Athletic socks
- ❑ Knee socks
- ❑ Panty hose
- ❑ Trouser socks

LINGERIE

- ❏ Bras
- ❏ Camisoles
- ❏ Long johns
- ❏ Panties
- ❏ Slips
- ❏ Sports bras
- ❏ Support garments

SLEEPWEAR

- ❏ Pajamas, nightgown
- ❏ Robe
- ❏ Slippers

FOR SPORTS

- ❏ Bathing suits
- ❏ Bathing suit cover-up
- ❏ Sports equipment
- ❏ Swim goggles
- ❏ Workout gear

FOR EVENING

- ❏ Dress, gown, or suit
- ❏ Evening bag
- ❏ Evening wrap, shawl
- ❏ Jewelry
- ❏ Lingerie
- ❏ Stockings

OUTERWEAR

- ❏ Baseball cap
- ❏ Gloves
- ❏ Overcoat
- ❏ Parka
- ❏ Raincoat, zip-out lining
- ❏ Sun hat
- ❏ Tote bag
- ❏ Umbrella
- ❏ Windbreaker
- ❏ Winter hat

Packing Pointers

▶ Active Trips and Adventures

On these trips, you may be carrying everything, so you may need to pack for portability. Most likely, your clothing should be unfussy and durable—style will be secondary to comfort.

If you are going with an adventure travel outfitter, you will probably be sent a suggested packing list before the trip. Often, the staff of these businesses are adventure lovers themselves who really know what works in the environment you'll be exploring. Don't be shy about calling to ask for advice on name brands and specific articles of clothing.

When assembling your wardrobe, remember that you'll want to dress in layers that can be put on and taken off as the temperature and your activity level warrant. This is true whether you're traveling in the mountains or the desert. Garments made of fleece such as Polartec, Polarfleece, and other microfibers are warm, lightweight, and easy to pack.

Perhaps the most important thing is a good pair of shoes. Depending on the trip, many adventure mavens suggest taking both sport sandals like Tevas (for fording rivers) and lightweight nylon hiking boots (for everything else, except truly off-the-trail rocky terrain, in which case serious leather boots are required). Know before you go about your chosen terrain. And please, please, please break the boots in before your trip!

Adventure trips require a more complete first-aid kit than the one suggested in Chapter 2. Compact yet fully stocked kits are available at sports retail stores.

TRAVEL AIDS YOU MAY WANT TO PACK

- ❏ Adapters, converter
- ❏ Alarm clock
- ❏ Audiotapes, CDs
- ❏ Batteries
- ❏ Binoculars
- ❏ Books on tape
- ❏ Calculator
- ❏ Camera, lenses, film
- ❏ Cassette/CD player
- ❏ Citronella candle
- ❏ Compass
- ❏ Earplugs
- ❏ Flashlight
- ❏ Guidebooks
- ❏ Luggage tags

- ❏ Luggage locks
- ❏ Maps
- ❏ Money belt
- ❏ Money converter
- ❏ Phrasebook
- ❏ Pillow
- ❏ Radio
- ❏ Sleep mask
- ❏ Travel iron
- ❏ Travel journal
- ❏ Video recorder, blank tapes
- ❏ Watchman
- ❏ Water bottle
- ❏ Water purification tablets

FOR THE DESERT That this dry and dusty environment calls for protection from the sun and the elements may come as no surprise. Depending on your activity, you'll need sturdy hiking boots to shield your feet from rocks underfoot. Loose-fitting, light-colored cotton or silk clothing is a must, preferably long-sleeve shirts and long pants that minimize sun exposure; a bandanna wards off dust and is useful to mop off your forehead when it's sweaty. Speaking of dust, be aware that it will get into every crevice of your camera and case and potentially jam

IDEAS FOR THE DESERT

❏ Anorak ❏ Film
❏ Bandanna ❏ Hiking boots
❏ Dust-proof camera case ❏ Insect repellent
❏ Cooler ❏ Sun hat
❏ Day pack ❏ Synthetic ice
❏ Casual cotton clothing ❏ Sweater or jacket
❏ Dressy outfit

it up—an underwater camera with tightly fitting gaskets is more secure than an ordinary point-and-shoot or 35mm model.

Less expected is the sudden downpour or windstorm, when you'll be glad to have an anorak (particularly one made of breathable fabric), and the sudden plummeting of temperatures when the sun goes down (which will send you straight to your tent in search of a sweater). Also, note that some package safari trips have an occasional dress-up evening; sequins and dinner jackets are not necessary, but a long skirt or sundress for women and khakis and a casual shirt for men would be appropriate. Your strategy should be to bring as little as possible, so you aren't weighed down by your bags.

If you're making short day hikes, you may want to pack a lightweight cooler and synthetic ice to keep film or drinks from getting overly warm.

FOR THE TROPICS AND FOR SUMMER You'll need much of the same gear you do in the desert—sun hat, sunscreen, insect repellent, and loose-fitting cotton or silk clothing, preferably long-sleeve shirts and long pants. In hot weather and hot climates, it's important to take good care of your feet. Shoes that allow your feet to breathe, such as sport sandals, are essential on the beach. In a rain forest or jungle, quick-drying socks and sturdy closed-toe shoes are a must as protection from insects and waterborne bacteria—consider lightweight hiking shoes made of canvas or open-weave nylon. You'll also need rain gear and, for any dress-up events, a sundress or silk blouse and trousers for women; a long-sleeve shirt and khakis for men.

On day trips take a small lightweight cooler and synthetic ice to carry film—either the film you tote with you on the trail or the film you've left behind in the car.

IDEAS FOR HOT WEATHER

- ❏ Anorak
- ❏ Antifungal foot powder
- ❏ Bandanna
- ❏ Cooler
- ❏ Cotton clothing
- ❏ Day pack
- ❏ Dressy outfit
- ❏ Film
- ❏ Hiking boots
- ❏ Insect repellent
- ❏ Sport sandals
- ❏ Socks
- ❏ Sun hat
- ❏ Synthetic ice
- ❏ Umbrella

FOR WINTER My friend Stephanie has some advice to people considering traveling in winter: Don't. She feels that bulky clothing translates into a packing nightmare.

Not necessarily. Remember the principle of dressing in layers. Next to your skin, wear long johns made of light silk or a moisture-wicking synthetic—leggings and a crew-neck or turtleneck. On top of that should go lighter, easy-to-pack T-shirts, turtlenecks, or long-sleeve shirts. Top it all off with a sweater or fleece pullover depending on the temperature, followed by your snowsuit or ski parka and snow pants.

Remember the old saying, "If your feet are cold, put on a hat"? To that should be added a warm fleece neck gaiter. On your feet, go with whatever is state-of-the-art in ski socks at the time of your trip: They should retain their insulating properties even when they're wet—recognize that they will get wet, and bring several pairs. You'll need them to fit underneath your ski boots or hiking boots as well as under your après-sport footgear. And when you're skiing, if all else fails, pick up one of those little hand- or foot-warming packets in the base lodge and experience instant, miraculous warmth.

You should also bring sunscreen and lip balm to protect against snow-reflected sun and wind burn. If your parka pockets aren't commodious, bring a fanny pack to stash this, your camera, extra film, and any other necessities, such as a pocket-size pack of tissues for blowing your nose or defogging your goggles or glasses. (Tip: If you're bringing film from home, get a relatively slow speed since sun on snow can generate a lot of light.)

If you're taking a ski vacation, don't forget to include warm clothing that will take you out to a nice dinner après-ski, including footwear for indoors and out with appropriate socks, driving gloves, a neck scarf, and a hat to wear between your lodging place and your dinner destination, and a layered outfit that won't leave you shivering while your car warms up (you may even take to wearing your long johns during every waking hour).

As for ski equipment, several of my friends like to send their skis and poles to their resort via overnight courier—it saves hassles at the airport. Invest in bags for your skis and boots. Some have enough room to pack a few extra garments, and they protect your skis from road salt when you drive between the airport or your home and your ski destination.

IDEAS FOR COLD WEATHER

- ❏ Driving gloves
- ❏ Fanny pack
- ❏ Fleece neck gaiter
- ❏ Fleece parka
- ❏ Fleece ear warmer
- ❏ Hats
- ❏ Lip balm
- ❏ Long johns
- ❏ Scarf
- ❏ Shoes to wear indoors
- ❏ Ski gloves or mittens
- ❏ Ski hat
- ❏ Ski parka
- ❏ Snow goggles
- ❏ Snow pants
- ❏ Snow boots
- ❏ Street clothes
- ❏ Sweaters
- ❏ Thermal socks
- ❏ Tissues, handkerchief
- ❏ Turtlenecks

FOR DAY HIKES IN THE MOUNTAINS On these you'll often pass through a series of microclimates in one afternoon; as soon as you get heated up through exertion, you can bet the temperature will fall. So make sure you have lots of layers, which you can lay on and peel off as temperatures dictate. In early spring and fall, when it's still chilly, start with synthetic underwear, next to your skin, the kind that wicks moisture away from your body (bring several sets). In warmer weather, wear quick-drying shorts or pants. (You'll want several sets of these, too.) You may then want a T-shirt or turtleneck, topped by a fleece vest and/or pullover and a windbreaker made of material that's waterproof yet breathable, such as Gore-Tex. In spring or fall, just in case, you may want to throw a hat and a fleece neck gaiter into your day pack, along with your water bottle and some high-energy trail snacks such as raisins, nuts, and chocolate. On your feet, you'll want socks with good cushioning properties to wear over wicking liner socks. And don't forget your camera. If your venture into the hills calls for river rafting or other watery activities, you may want to go shopping for a camera that can handle more than the occasional splash.

Finally, if your trip calls for a return to civilization (or in case you'll be day-hiking and returning to a cozy ranch or B&B at the end of every day), be sure to include street clothes, including shoes and socks. If you have any thoughts of a nice dinner out during your trip or at either end, plan accordingly.

IDEAS FOR MOUNTAIN TRIPS

❑ Anorak	❑ Insect repellent
❑ Bandanna	❑ Extra laces
❑ Water-resistant camera	❑ Liner socks
❑ Day pack	❑ Long johns
❑ Fleece gloves	❑ Street clothes
❑ Fleece neck gaiter	❑ Thick socks
❑ Fleece pullover	❑ Trousers or shorts
❑ Fleece vest	❑ Turtleneck or T-shirt
❑ Hiking boots	❑ Warm hat

ABOUT YOUR LUGGAGE A trip in the great outdoors requires rugged luggage that can take a beating from the elements. In these circumstances, waterproofing is critical—think of a river-rafting trip, or imagine your bags being strapped to the top of a safari bus during a storm. Then, too, you'll need pieces that allow you to pack a minimum amount of stuff with the most portability. Duffels and travel packs really answer the call for situations like this. Both provide enough protection for the type of clothing you'll pack.

IDEAS FOR YOUR DAY PACK

❏ Binoculars	❏ Map
❏ Camera, film	❏ Matches
❏ Compass	❏ Pocket knife
❏ Extra clothing	❏ Snacks
❏ First-aid kit	❏ Sunglasses
❏ Flashlight	❏ Sunscreen
❏ Insect repellent	❏ Water bottle, filled

A day pack is essential on many kinds of adventure trips. In it, you'll want to store extra clothing appropriate for the weather and the climate: a bathing suit, an extra T-shirt, a waterproof parka, mittens and a hat, a spare pair of socks. A small flashlight can come in handy: check the bulb and batteries and replace them if necessary. Depending on the nature of your trip, you may also want to include signaling devices such as flares or a whistle.

▶ Business Trips and Seminars

Whether it's a convention, a conference, a sales call, an interview, or a high-level brainstorming session, you're traveling for business, not pleasure. Striking the right professional appearance can help you careerwise, so pack thoughtfully.

KNOW THE CUSTOMS Choose conservative suits or casual professional clothing, depending on the customs of your field of business and the business activities you anticipate (roll-up-the-sleeves seminars as opposed to client presentations, for example). Find out the local business customs for the city you're going to. The open-collar shirt that's appropriate in Singapore will cost you points in London.

Meeting new people? Err on the side of the conservative—a loud tie or low-cut blouse could create a disastrous first impression.

HOW TO PACK LESS Look over your itinerary to decide whether you will meet different people (fresh sales prospects, perhaps) each day or see the same colleagues over and over. This will dictate the number of outfits you'll need.

On a short trip, men may be able to get by with one suit—just change the color of your shirt and tie each day. If you're dressing more casually, you can pair a single sweater or blazer with different pants or skirts and shirts each day. Opt for an unobtrusive style, and chances are that your clients or associates won't focus on the fact that you're repeating the outfit.

Because accidents will happen, pack one or two extra shirts or blouses and pairs of panty hose. On a recent business trip my cousin Mike spilled coffee all over himself and was thrilled he had an extra shirt. And, on the subject of the unanticipated, you may find it worth your while to tuck in a compact folding umbrella.

PLAN FOR DOWNTIME Women may want to pack one dressy outfit as well, especially if their business attire is very conservative. Men can still get by with a daytime suit at dinner, unless there's a black-tie event on the agenda.

Bring some smart casual clothing if you'll be with colleagues rather than on your own after work. This can be valuable bonding time that will enhance your working relationships—remaining in a suit may make you seem standoffish.

Just because you're traveling on business doesn't mean you can't exercise; in fact, it may help you de-stress. Most hotels have pools, exercise rooms, or both, so pack your swimsuit or a pair of shorts and T-shirt.

FITNESS TO GO

Both business and leisure travelers like to incorporate a bit of a workout into their daily routine while on the road, and most hotels have answered this need with on-site health spas and pools. Easy-to-pack equipment for a hotel-room workout might include a Walkman with energizing tapes, industrial-size rubber bands for resistance exercises, inflatable bags or empty plastic bottles to fill with water and use as hand weights, or a jump rope. Most exercise clothing is made of fabric that dries quickly, so if you have packed some liquid detergent, you can bring one set of clothing and wash it after each use. Or skip the equipment and simply take along a bathing suit for the hotel pool.

DON'T FORGET ABOUT YOUR FEET If you're heading to a meeting or trade show where you'll be standing for hours at a time, make sure the shoes you bring are comfortable—flats are a good idea for women. One woman executive advises packing a pair of slippers, which she puts on after a day in the exhibit hall.

ABOUT YOUR LUGGAGE Business travelers find that garment bags and wheeled pullmans are most convenient for their needs. They do the best job protecting formal clothing, and the pieces add their own bit of polish to your appearance, allowing you to look organized and professional.

▶ Casual Vacations

Casual vacations, such as a weekend trip to a bed-and-breakfast or a quaint small hotel in the country, require clothing suited to your activities.

THE SPORTING LIFE For specific sports such as golf and tennis, bring appropriate clothes and footwear; call ahead to see if you can rent equipment at your destination. (You'll want to call ahead anyway to reserve tee times or court times.)

If country walks are on your to-do list, be sure you've got the right shoes. And if you're going into tall grass or woods in tick country—for bird-watching, perhaps—be sure to pack long pants, socks, and long-sleeve shirts.

If you're bike touring, don't forget your helmet and bike clothing. Be sure to include at least one waterproof layer and a thermal layer underneath if the weather's likely to get cold. Depending on when and where you plan to cycle, you may want to acquire a light for night riding, spare tire tubes and a patch kit, cycling gloves, and a water bottle if you don't already have them. Ditto for a good lock—you will need to leave your bike at some point, if only to go inside a store to replenish your drink supply. Even if you're carrying all your gear on your bike, consider bringing at least one set of street clothes and a pair of regular shoes so that you can go out to dinner without looking like a straggler from the Tour de France.

For horseback riding, toss in jeans and shoes with heels—or, if you have them, your jodhpurs, helmet, and riding boots. Helmets and boots take up a lot of luggage room, but if you're a serious rider you may consider them worth the space.

Casual trips are often car trips—so you can haul more stuff, even leaving some locked in your trunk overnight if you're changing hotels each day. This allows you to include more sports gear—snowshoes as well as skis, for example, or snorkels and fins as well as a beach umbrella. Just don't get the car so loaded down that there's no room for you.

DRESS FOR THE WEATHER Spring, fall, or summer, a windbreaker is handy. Look for one that's waterproof, has lots of pockets, and can be rolled into a tiny pouch. In winter, a fleece pullover does the same duty. Not only does a light jacket bridge all sorts of weather changes, the pockets are handy for carrying odds and ends, including a camera, wallet, map, guidebook, and water bottle. For short excursions you may be able to do without a day pack or purse if you've got a big front pouch in your jacket.

GOING ANTIQUING? Stay away from long, sweeping skirts, wide-brimmed hats, and bulky jackets, which can wreak havoc in narrow-aisled shops full of expensive breakables. You'll probably have large items shipped home, but toss some bubble wrap in your luggage when you pack, and leave room in your carry-on for small items, safely swaddled.

EATING OUT On a weekend trip, you'll need fewer clothes for fewer days, so pruning your wardrobe is less of a problem. If you plan to be out sightseeing and playing sports by day, it may be worth it to bring a change of clothes for dinner each night. It'll make dinner out seem more of a treat and will give you the illusion of a longer, fuller, yet more relaxed day.

When researching your trip, find out if there's a superb restaurant in the area that you'd like to try. Call ahead for reservations, and pack at least one dressy outfit for the big night.

ABOUT YOUR LUGGAGE For a quick casual vacation, opt for a suitcase with wheels or a duffel bag, depending on how you prefer to carry your luggage. Both provide adequate protection for sporty casual clothing, and the duffel can take one or two fancier garments without creasing chaos. Choose a bag on the small side, since you often have to carry your own bags at B&Bs. Also consider taking a lightweight duffel for sports gear.

▶ City Vacations

Cities are inherently more formal than resorts or rural areas, but unless you're there on business, your style can be relatively casual. Remember above all that cities have stores; shopping may in fact be part of your itinerary. Anything you decide not to pack can be bought later at your destination.

BE KIND TO YOUR TOOTSIES Sightseeing usually requires lots of walking on pavement; in Europe this may even mean cobblestones. A pair of sturdy, comfortable, flat-heeled shoes is a must. Don't choose sandals, which let your feet get grimy and don't protect your toes. To make shoes do double duty, men may want to buy a pair of brogues or loafers, which are comfortable for walking yet look presentable when paired with a suit or sport jacket.

SAY CHEESE! Speaking of sightseeing—it usually requires a camera. Don't forget it.

KNOW LOCAL DO'S AND TABOOS Get acquainted with that city's customs and traditions. Milan may be the Italian design capital, but women are still expected to cover their bare shoulders with a scarf when entering the city's famous cathedral.

You needn't dress as formally as you might expect. After all, you're a tourist. So even though businesspeople in the same city wear suits, shorts are perfectly okay for summer sightseeing in many areas—but again, check your guidebook to ascertain local customs.

LAYER, LAYER, LAYER If you're the sort who likes to be out and about all day, anticipate changes in temperature. On a recent summer trip to San Francisco, Wendy was very glad she'd brought light jackets for herself and her two kids—they needed them in the chilly morning fog and after dinner, even though afternoon highs were in the 70s. Even where the weather is uniformly warm, remember that indoor museums and shopping malls may be frigidly air-conditioned.

PLAN FOR AFTER DARK Keep in mind what you'll be doing at night—if you'll be attending evening performances of the opera or ballet, or sampling an elegant restaurant, include one more dressy outfit. One should be enough, though, if you won't be seeing the same people night after night.

BRING AN UMBRELLA Observe the Boy Scout's motto, and be prepared!

PRECAUTIONS Women should wear a minimum of jewelry. Flashy finery only attracts trouble. And even if you don't normally wear a money belt or security pouch, you should consider doing so in cities.

ABOUT YOUR LUGGAGE For your urban vacation, you might wish to mix and match your luggage: Take a lightweight garment bag for a few dressy outfits and a small suitcase with wheels for the rest of your gear.

▶ Cruises

A cruise vacation requires several types of clothing and perhaps a bit more of it than other trips. That's fine, because after you've unpacked you won't even see your bags again until it's time to disembark. Most cruise lines issue a list of suggested clothing for time on board and ashore.

FOR SHORE EXCURSIONS Bring casual, sporty clothing with a conservative slant for shore excursions—leave tank tops and miniskirts on the ship. Layers are always a good idea. *See* "Traveling in the Tropics and in Summer," *below.* For an Alaska cruise, a good jacket, hat, and gloves are a must, even in August. You'll also be glad to have a water bottle that you can slip into your day pack.

Good walking shoes, broken in before the trip, are best for shore excursions, whether you'll be strolling on cobblestones or clambering over Maya ruins.

For all climates, you'll need a sun hat or other head covering: You don't want to be forced to waste your brief time in port by taking a midday siesta in the shade. And don't forget your camera and film—and a compact folding umbrella, just in case.

SWIMMING, SPORTS You'll need bathing suits, cover-ups, and sunscreen for the sun deck and pool. And bring sports equipment if your cruise's scheduled port stops allow access to tennis courts and golf courses.

FORMAL NIGHTS, AFTER DARK The cruise line's suggested clothing list will spell out how many formal nights to expect. For a typical week-long cruise, you can count on at least two. For these evenings, women are expected to wear an evening dress, men a dark suit or tuxedo. Break out the sequins, taffeta, and tulle—a cruise may be the one time you can wear that bridesmaid's dress again.

The theme evenings scheduled by some cruises are more fun if you get into the spirit. Find out what's planned for your cruise and pack something to go with it—berets for French night or Hawaiian shirts for a Polynesian evening, for example.

On most other evenings, dress is semiformal, which means a dress or pants suit for women; a sport jacket, tie, and slacks for men. Casual evenings, generally the first and last nights on board, call for neat-looking street clothes. Most ships do not permit shorts at dinner in the formal dining room.

Women should bring a light wrap to wear in air-conditioned rooms and for after-dinner stargazing on deck.

PRECAUTIONS In many ports, local thieves and pick-pockets consider cruise passengers prime game. Safeguard your valuables: Don't flaunt money, your passport, expensive camera equipment, or jewelry.

ABOUT YOUR LUGGAGE Pack formal clothing in a garment bag and the rest in a suitcase or duffel. Take along a day pack for shore excursions—it's helpful for toting water, an extra sweater, a camera, and film, among other essentials.

▶ For Families

When traveling with a family, your packing needs vary with the age of the child. This list progresses from infant necessities to older children's needs—keep revisiting it as your kids grow up.

If the water supply at your destination is iffy, bring canned baby formula. You may also want to bring your child's car seat. Rental car companies can provide one but only by advance arrangement, and you may not like what you get. On airplanes, as in cars, babies and toddlers are safer in a car seat. Unfortunately, this can be an expensive proposition: children under two fly free if they sit on your lap (and are often permitted to ride in their car seats at no extra cost when space is available), but parents who haven't bought their youngsters a ticket must hold their offspring on their lap on a flight that's full.

If you're flying, you can't count on meal service at the hours your children will want to be fed. Check to see what will be served, pack accordingly—or risk tantrums (yours, at the flight attendants). Stick with no-sugar snacks, and store them in resealable sandwich bags or small plastic tubs with snap-on lids; refillable sports bottles make a good alternative to juice boxes.

Holly, mother of three, always packs a spare bath towel— useful for cleaning up spills and, until then, as a blanket. Her kids are active, so she always brings two swimsuits per child, so there's always a dry one to slip into. (And she brings them along on every trip, just in case!) In case of temperature changes, Wendy slips in one out-of-season outfit for each of her two sons—long pants in summer, shorts in spring and fall.

Check on whether you'll have a VCR in your hotel room or can rent one. You'll never catch me bringing a VCR— vacation is a great time to take a break from TV. But some families traveling by car in the States do put one to use at their destination, or even in the car. If you want to join them, bring a favorite videotape or two.

BAG 'EM

TIP

Samsonite has a nifty tip for parents: organize toddlers' clothes into outfits—tops, bottoms, socks, and underwear—and put each outfit into its own resealable plastic bag. Makes getting dressed in the AM a cinch.

ABOUT YOUR LUGGAGE Duffels are well suited for packing kids' clothes, since wrinkles are generally not an

KID STUFF

FOR KIDS IN DIAPERS

- ❏ Diapers
- ❏ Baby wipes
- ❏ Diaper-rash cream
- ❏ Baby powder
- ❏ Changing pad
- ❏ Two outfits and pajamas per day

FOR BOTTLE KIDS

- ❏ Baby formula
- ❏ Bottles or holders and liners
- ❏ Bottle nipples
- ❏ Rings
- ❏ Bottle caps
- ❏ Bottle brush

FOR MOBILITY

- ❏ Car seat
- ❏ Baby carrier
- ❏ Collapsible stroller

COMFORTS

- ❏ Pacifiers and spares
- ❏ Your child's lovey
- ❏ A night-light

DIVERSIONS

- ❏ A ball
- ❏ Clipboard and paper
- ❏ Markers and crayons
- ❏ Sand toys
- ❏ Travel games
- ❏ Toy tote (see Chapter 2)
- ❏ VCR
- ❏ Favorite videotapes

FEEDING TIME

- ❏ Snacks
- ❏ Drinks
- ❏ Paper towels
- ❏ Baby wipes
- ❏ Terrycloth towel

FOR OLDER KIDS

- ❏ One outfit per day
- ❏ Two extra tops
- ❏ An extra pair of pants
- ❏ Two swimsuits per child
- ❏ Swim goggles
- ❏ One nice outfit for dress
- ❏ An out-of-season outfit
- ❏ Sweatshirt, sweater
- ❏ Windbreaker

JUST IN CASE

- ❏ Medications your child may need
- ❏ Thermometer
- ❏ Tylenol
- ❏ Your pediatrician's phone number

issue. If you've got small children, though, a travel pack may be a better bet, since it leaves parents' hands free to push a stroller or hold a child's hand. When packing, include some garments belonging to each family member in every suitcase—this way, if one bag goes missing, you'll all still have something to wear. Give each walking child his or her own small backpack for en route snacks and toys. Don't, however, expect young children to handle their own carry-on suitcases; better to check one large bag and have fewer pieces of luggage to track.

▌ Resort Vacations

Here, the object is to get away and relax. But even Florida, Hawaii, the Caribbean, and Mexico have their own codes of dress and behavior.

GET SAVVY ABOUT SPORTS GEAR Know in advance what sports are offered at your resort, and for everything you plan to do, come with appropriate attire, including footwear—golf shoes, tennis shoes, aqua socks, whatever you'll need. Few resorts require tennis whites, but it's a good idea to bring them; white clothes are cooler in the sun anyway. If there's horseback riding on site, pack a pair of jeans and shoes with heels.

Call the resort to find out what equipment you can rent on site, then decide whether you want to bring your own.

If water sports are a mainstay, bring two bathing suits so you can wear one while the other's drying.

You may spend the day in a bathing suit and T-shirt or cover-up. But women should save short shorts and microminidresses for the pool or resort grounds. Walking shorts and polo shirts, T-shirts, or sundresses are better suited for shopping in town. For daytime sightseeing, men may wear T-shirts or polo shirts, shorts, and either sneakers and socks or boat shoes without socks.

WHAT'S UP WHEN THE SUN GOES DOWN? In the evening, depending on the formality of the resort or restaurant, men might want to switch to a long-sleeve shirt or polo shirt and long pants, either jeans or khakis. Jackets and ties are seldom required—call the resort in advance to be sure. Women can wear anything from a top and skirt to a chic cotton pants suit or a pretty sundress, short or long. If you have a brochure from your resort, one glance at its photos should clue you in to the formality level.

HANDY BRING-ALONGS Don't forget a camera and a couple of rolls of film. And consider throwing in a roomy tote bag as a convenient, if not totally secure, place to stash it poolside. Finally, don't forget sunscreen (it'll be cheaper at home) and, if you're at all sensitive to the sun, a sun hat.

PRECAUTIONS On resort trips, as in the city, it's best to avoid unnecessary displays of jewelry and cash.

ABOUT YOUR LUGGAGE What you'll pack for a resort destination depends on where you're headed and the level of formality you expect there. At casual places you can roll all your clothing into a duffel bag. If you're staying at a more formal property, you may opt for a light-weight garment bag for fancier clothing and a suitcase on wheels for the rest.

4

HOW TO PACK
FOR
THE WAY BACK

"To ship to the United States, that will be $70," the salesclerk said. It was 1987. I was standing at Lladrós "R" Us in Toledo, Spain, and I was not happy. Having just negotiated a great price for a delicate Lladró figurine, I had nonchalantly asked about shipping. But on my student budget, $70 was out of the question. "No, thanks," I said. "I'll carry it myself." I heard one of my friends groan.

Understand that this was the first week of a four-week backpacking tour of Europe via Eurail, with stops in Spain, France, Monaco, and Italy. And I don't think I need to remind you about my backpack situation (*see* Chapter 1). But I have loyal friends who indulge my whims. Together, we covered the blue Lladró box with a brown plastic bag, then tied the box securely to the bottom of my backpack, in between two of the exposed aluminum frame pipes, where it hung for the next few weeks. I am pleased to report that the figurine arrived home safely. (Perhaps it was all those candles I lighted in Italy.) But had my lovely uninsured Lladró broken when I collapsed under the weight of my backpack in Rome, I would have had no recourse. If I could do it again, I'd ship the darn thing.

Whether you're traveling for business or pleasure, the odds are you're going to accumulate material of one kind or another. Having a strategy for dealing with it is a wise idea and will make your return trip easier.

▶ Use Your Packing List

Here's hoping you followed the advice in Chapters 2 and 3 to write down your packing list and keep a copy. (And you did remember to cross off all those items you wisely decided at the last minute to leave at home, didn't you?) If you did, repacking should be a no-sweat process. By checking each item off the list as it is packed, you reduce the risk of leaving something behind.

This is especially useful if you've been staying in one place for a number of days—getting settled usually involves dispersing your belongings in various drawers and closets. And if you're traveling with a family, you can't count on your memory to make sure you've retrieved every little car and animal from under the beds, let alone make sure your child's beloved stuffed friend isn't hidden in the bedding.

Even if you've been changing hotels daily, virtually living out of your suitcase, double-checking the list is a good way to streamline the constant packing.

▶ Dirty Laundry

There's one major difference between the clothes you brought with you and the clothes you're taking home: On the way home, probably all your clothes will be dirty. That is, if you didn't pack way too many extra outfits. (If you did, remember this next time you get ready for a trip.)

Experienced travelers often bring a laundry bag, even if it's only a plastic trash bag, to keep the clothes they've already worn separate from fresh clothes. For long trips, count on a few visits to the laundromat, or use hotel laundry services to get more wear out of your travel wardrobe. If you'll be using a laundromat, bring a laundry bag strong enough to tote your dirty duds securely.

PACK BACKWARD

TIP

Arizona businesswoman Patricia Kincaid earned kudos as one of the country's savviest women business travelers for her advice to pack backward. Take everything out of your suitcase on arrival, and put it back in as you wear it. You'll eliminate the last-minute rush to repack.

Remember how hard you had to work back home to fit everything into your suitcase in the first place? Balled-up dirty laundry will not occupy the same suitcase space as your carefully folded, rolled, or interlocked clean clothes. So dump out that dirty laundry and spread it flat, one piece at a time, in a stack in the bottom of your suitcase—if you've got a duffel you may want to re-roll it. Around the corners tuck your shoes, stuffed with dirty socks and underwear. (Use shoe bags even though your clothes are dirty, or risk stains from any grease or tar that may be on the soles.) Break out those extra plastic bags you packed and bundle up anything that's damp so that it doesn't generate mildew in the rest of your clothing. Put the laundry bag on top, and then pack your remaining clothes. This procedure keeps clean and soiled stuff separate; when you get home, whatever is clean can go straight into your dresser or closet, while the rest heads for the laundry hamper.

If you're repacking a garment bag, of course, you'll have to hang up your dirty clothes. If possible, put them in the front of the bag, where they will cushion your clean garments and help keep them from wrinkling. Use any remaining plastic dry-cleaner bags to separate clean and dirty garments.

▶ The Paper Chase

I am convinced that no one understands the weight of paper in quite the way a travel journalist does. A single morning of hotel site inspections often yields six or eight hefty press kits; the paper accumulated during a five-day jaunt could fill an extra suitcase. And yet there's always the possibility that one of those brochures or releases will contain the pertinent fact that makes an article sing. What's a writer to do?

This same problem is shared by many business travelers— conference materials, marketing reports, brochures collected on the trade-show floor, all have a way of stacking up on the desk in your hotel room.

KEEP IT UNDER CONTROL Try to consolidate the pile daily, even if it means staying awake an extra half hour each evening to do so. Discard exterior folders, weed out duplicate information. Leaf through any particularly bulky documents to digest whatever sections are pertinent to you; tear out only the relevant pages, or jot down on a sheet of hotel stationery any facts you may need to retrieve later, so you can throw away the document.

SHIP IT HOME If the pile is really huge, see if you can ship it: Some writers mail (or express mail) printed material home to the office or house. Here's where the 10" x 13" manila envelopes in your portable office come in handy. One lawyer I know keeps in touch with his office while on vacation by having his secretary send a continual flow of briefs and court documents via overnight mail; it took a while before he realized that he should also have her supply him with a handful of filled-out overnight-mail vouchers so that he could wing the whole batch back to his desk at the end of the trip.

SHIP OR SCHLEP If shipping isn't possible, you have only one option: Carry it home. If, at the moment of packing, you can envision this situation, put in the extra tote bag I recommended to passionate shoppers in Chapter 2. Or pack your papers flat in your luggage, but remember that they will add quite a bit of weight to the bag, and you may not be able to lift it over your head into the overhead compartment of an airplane if you have to. Prepare to ask for help or store it under the seat in front of you.

▶ Souvenir Savvy

During one memorable trip to Italy, my mother—a dedicated shopper—bought a marble chessboard and chessmen, two porcelain plates, an alabaster candlestick, three prints, various odds and ends of jewelry, and a painted mask from Venice. When the lock broke on her suitcase at the airport (marble can be rather tough on luggage), a kind man at Alitalia tied a stout rope around the bag and sent it on. In this case, my mom's mistake was not that she had bought too much, but that she hadn't anticipated her need for extra packing space on the return trip.

I've learned the hard way about several ways to bring back souvenirs and gifts from afar without having an international packing incident.

TIPS FROM AN ANONYMOUS BAGGAGE HANDLER

Luggage truly takes a beating. It gets slammed into a dirty taxi trunk, thrown down onto the pavement in front of the airport terminal, then tossed onto a conveyor belt headed straight for...you guessed it, the baggage handlers. Ever wonder what life is really like behind those partitions? So did I—so I did a little research. Here's the word from the guys themselves:

• "Buy soft-sided luggage. Hard-sided luggage tends to split open when thrown—excuse me, dropped—onto baggage carts and conveyor belts. Soft-sided luggage can take impact better."

• "Stay within airline limits on weight, size, etc. If your luggage is heavier than it should be, you may fool the ticket agent, but we bagmen will not thank you for it, and your poor luggage will surely pay."

• "Sorry, folks, but sometimes all a piece of luggage has to do is to look different—either in color, height, or size—to be singled out for abuse."

• "Bags that 'misbehave' are definitely going to get it. I have actually heard an associate of mine explain, 'The duffel got mean with me, so I got mean back.'"

• "Label all your luggage with your name and telephone number, both inside and out. Outside luggage tags are the first casualties."

• "While you're at it, pull off all those old luggage tags from your last trip. It really frosts me when people complain about a misdirected suitcase when there are tags for three different airports on the handle."

• "If your suitcase has detachable handles or straps, take them off before you check in. Some of my guys collect them and use 'em as dog leashes."

DON'T BUY WHAT WON'T FIT IN YOUR SUITCASE
The key is sometimes as simple as scale. Good things
come in small packages: Choose small items such as earrings or other jewelry. Prints are always good—they can
be placed in an envelope for protection and packed flat, at
least if you use a pullman. Scarves, ties, and sarongs make
wonderful souvenirs and add almost no weight. T-shirts
are good, too.

ANTICIPATE SHOPPING FRENZIES If you know
that you tend to fall helpless when your acquisitive im-
pulses get going, simply pack an empty suitcase when you
pack your clothing: Some shopaholics and other travel
mavens actually fit the smaller suitcase inside the larger
one on the outgoing trip.

THE SHIPPING OPTION Please—please!—remember that sending your purchases home is always an option.
If you insure the package and it is damaged, you will be
reimbursed.

U.S. Customs permits travelers to send packages home
duty-free: up to $200 worth of goods for personal use, with
a limit of one parcel per addressee per day (and no alco-
hol or tobacco products or perfume worth more than $5).
So if you see during your trip that you're getting close to
the $400 limit, sort through your stuff and see what you
can mail. Mark the package PERSONAL USE, and attach a
list of its contents and their retail value. Do not label the
package UNSOLICITED GIFT, or your duty-free exemption
will drop to $100. Most reputable stores will handle the
mailing for you. Your best choices are bulky or heavy items
that will fit less readily in your luggage on the return trip.

ABOUT TRANSPORTING LIQUOR Have liquor
packed by the merchant in a cardboard carrier—it's a lot
easier to transport and show to customs. And always bring
champagne aboard with you—it needs the pressurized air
of the cabin.

▶ At Customs

Frequent overseas travelers know that certain techniques can eliminate at least some of the hassles when leaving your destination and arriving back in the United States.

KEEP RECEIPTS CLOSE AT HAND If you've been abroad, use one of the manila envelopes or resealable plastic bags from your portable office to hold receipts of purchases you've made. On the way home, keep the receipts where they're handy, with your travel documents. This will make things a lot easier if you're applying for an exemption from value-added taxes (VAT) in your host country—always a good idea, since VATs of 15% or 20% can really add up on expensive items. Check your travel guide regarding procedures for the country you're visiting. In most countries, you need to get a special VAT-exempt invoice at the point of purchase, then present it to customs officials at your point of departure; your sales tax refund will be mailed to you later, or you may be given a voucher that will allow you to collect the rebate at an airport bank branch before you leave the country.

The envelope of receipts will also come in handy when you pass through U.S. Customs on your way home. Keep it with you on the plane so you can fill out your customs declaration card in flight. Try to pack purchases in one bag, if possible—again, this saves time should you be asked to present them for inspection.

Packing List

Packing List

Packing List

Packing List

Packing List

Packing List

Packing List